# SUPERSTAR O...
# OF ANTI-HERO...

**His first law is that of survival.**

**He doesn't trust flowery words or make fine moral distinctions.**

**Action he thrives on, immediate results are what he demands.**

This is the character portrayed by Clint Eastwood—the character that has captured the imagination of the world.

How does Eastwood relate to this character? How has the character changed over the years? What may the future bring?

In interviews with Clint Eastwood himself, with the actors, actresses, writers, and directors who have worked with him, and in careful viewings of all the movies* he has made, you will gain new insight into the most elusive superstar of them all—

# CLINT EASTWOOD

*Including a complete Filmography at the back of the book.*

# Other SIGNET Film Personality Books

☐ **BOGIE: The Biography of Humphrey Bogart by Joe Hyams; with an Introduction by Lauren Bacall.** BOGIE does more than report events. It relives a life. The brawls, the sprees, the razor-edged wisecracks: Hyams describes them all. He recaptures the deep friendships —with Spencer Tracy, Judy Garland, Katharine Hepburn. He probes Bogart's stormy youth; his stubborn climb to stardom; his three rocky marital adventures and his last happy marriage to Lauren Bacall.
(#Y5404—$1.25)

☐ **MR. LAUREL AND MR. HARDY by John McCabe.** "An affectionate and perceptive dual profile," said **The New York Times** of this biography of two of the greatest comedians of all time. Abundantly illustrated with photographs. With a special foreword by comedian Dick Van Dyke. (#Y5021—$1.25)

☐ **SPENCER TRACY by Larry Swindell.** In this first biography ever written about the actor, we see Spencer Tracy as he really was—gruff, intensely emotional and completely honest. We see him with his cronies and his long personal and professional relationship with Katharine Hepburn. A complete listing of every film he did and an Index is included. "Meticulous portrait . . . it gives us all the dimensions . . . of a rare, real giant of yesterday's picture parade."—New York Times Book Review (#Q4486—95¢)

☐ **DRAT! W. C. Fields' Picture Book, edited by Richard J. Anobile.** Introduction by Ed McMahon. DRAT is the encapsulate view, and what a view! of the greatest comedian of the century. Here, in happy juxtaposition of photos and quotes is the irreverent irrelevancy of W. C. Fields, the man and the actor. (#Q3933—95¢)

---

THE NEW AMERICAN LIBRARY, INC.,
P.O. Box 999, Bergenfield, New Jersey 07621

Please send me the SIGNET BOOKS I have checked above. I am enclosing $_____(check or money order—no currency or C.O.D.'s). Please include the list price plus 25¢ a copy to cover handling and mailing costs. (Prices and numbers are subject to change without notice.)

Name_____

Address_____

City_____State_____Zip Code_____
Allow at least 3 weeks for delivery

# CLINT EASTWOOD

## Stuart M. Kaminsky

SIGNET FILM SERIES

A SIGNET BOOK
NEW AMERICAN LIBRARY
TIMES MIRROR

Photo credits and acknowledgments: Universal Pictures;
Warner Brothers; The Malpaso Company; Paramount Pictures;
Metro-Goldwyn-Mayer; CBS Television; Cinefantastique;
Film Fan Monthly

SIGNET TRADEMARK REG. U.S. PAT. OFF. AND FOREIGN COUNTRIES
REGISTERED TRADEMARK—MARCA REGISTRADA
HECHO EN CHICAGO, U.S.A.

SIGNET, SIGNET CLASSICS, MENTOR, PLUME AND MERIDIAN BOOKS
are published by The New American Library, Inc.,
1301 Avenue of the Americas, New York, New York 10019

FIRST PRINTING, NOVEMBER, 1974

1 2 3 4 5 6 7 8 9

PRINTED IN THE UNITED STATES OF AMERICA

# To Peter

# ACKNOWLEDGMENTS

This book exists because of the encouragement and support of Leonard Maltin, the criticism of Merle Kaminsky, and the cooperation of dozens of people, especially Donald Siegel and Eli Wallach. Although my thanks also go to Clint Eastwood, I must make it clear that the book is in no way an official biography. Mr. Eastwood did not feel that the year 1974 was the right time for an authorized book, because, as he indicated to the author, "I still have many things to do" and "right now time would be prohibitive." I also wish to thank Kathy Esselman for her suggestions and ideas about Clint Eastwood and *Rawhide*, and Frank Jackson for his contributions and ideas about the Leone-directed films. Finally, my thanks go to Ingrid Kalessa for typing the manuscript.

# Contents

# Introduction

For several years Clint Eastwood has been the top movie star in the world. Or, put another way, his films have earned more money and drawn more people to theaters around the world than those that star any other actor. As popular as he is in the United States, he is even more popular in such diverse countries as Italy and Japan.

In spite of this, the public and his fans know very little about Eastwood as an actor, as a human being, and more recently, as a businessman and director. Part of this is a result of Eastwood's personality. Although he grants interviews and willingly publicizes his films, he is a man of few words. In addition, although he responds concisely to questions put to him, he seldom volunteers any information.

As with many major stars before him, there has been an air of mystery about his life and career. Where did he come from? How did he get into films? Does he have a family? Is he like the characters he portrays? What does he think about the films he has made? What does he want to do in his films? Who are his friends?

This book is an attempt to trace Eastwood's life

and career and to answer these and other questions. It is also an attempt to follow the development of the creation of a superstar, to see how his screen image has changed, discover how, in fact, he creates.

To get the story of Clint Eastwood, the author interviewed Eastwood and many people who have worked with him, including director Don Siegel, actor Eli Wallach, actresses Susan Clark and Elizabeth Hartman, writer Dean Riesner, editor Carl Pingatore, Universal Studios vice-president Jennings Lang, composer Lalo Schifrin, assistant director/production manager Joe Cavalier, and many others.

The author has also seen all of Eastwood's films at least once, and, as in the case of *Dirty Harry* and *Coogan's Bluff*, literally dozens of times. He has also read several hundred reviews and dozens of articles on Eastwood.

Since Eastwood is an active director and actor, any contemporary book on him cannot include his latest works. This book takes his life and career through *Magnum Force,* in which he starred, and *Breezy,* which he directed.

# CHAPTER ONE

# The Ultimate Antihero

Clint Eastwood is in training. He has been in training for more than twenty years, and that means running several miles each day when he can, doing push-ups, playing tennis, and watching what he eats. "A lot of actors don't condition themselves to long periods of hard physical effort," Eastwood once said. "Toward the end of the day, it shows in their performances."

For Eastwood, each new film, each step in his career, is a physical challenge for which he prepares like an athlete. His physical conditioning and careful diet are related to the fear he has always felt that he may be one step away from oblivion. His only weakness, if it is one, is a love of beer, preferably Olympia beer, which Dirty Harry Callahan drinks in *Magnum Force*, as does Thunderbolt in *Thunderbolt and Lightfoot*. "There are certain things," says Eastwood, "you just can't sacrifice."

The film production company that he began, Malpaso, has a name that is a cautious reminder of the ease with which one can fail in Hollywood. Although the name specifically refers to some property Eastwood owns on Malpaso Creek in

California, *malpaso* in Spanish means "bad step" or "misstep." Eastwood, like other stars before him, has carried the belief that the next film might be the last, that the fame he has achieved might suddenly vanish. The fear dwindles as success continues, but it probably never disappears.

Now that the six-foot-four-inch superstar is the world's number-one box-office attraction and an established director—*Play Misty for Me, High Plains Drifter, Breezy*—the gnawing doubt is not as much a part of his life, but Eastwood plans to keep what he has and build it further.

To do this, he works. He is actor, producer, director, businessman, public-relations man, and stunt man, but foremost, he is an actor.

Clint Eastwood the actor and the character he portrays on the screen did not suddenly spring forth in an Italian Western in 1974. The soft-spoken Eastwood cultivated his cool image through the late 1950's and early 1960's, developing his reserved acting style and creating the ultimate antihero. There are others in the same mold—Charles Bronson, Steve McQueen, James Coburn—but none has the international appeal of Eastwood, the man of few words off screen and on, the man who has created the image of the hero who looks out for himself first, is never taken in by emotion or women (except in *The Beguiled*), is sometimes hurt physically, but is never touched emotionally.

The screen image of Clint Eastwood antihero was nurtured by Eastwood the actor through years of television and a number of little-known films before *A Fistful of Dollars*. Certainly, a major part of the Eastwood character's appeal is his

4

physical appearance. He is the tall, strong all-American who seldom smiles, but when he does, it is private and cynical. He is perverse and handsome, a worldly-wise loner with no friends. To earn even a thimbleful of his respect in a film is a major assignment for a character. The character he portrays developed gradually and is still evolving.

"The idea of purposely setting out to change your image is a futile effort on the part of most actors who have become stars on the basis of what they do best," according to Eastwood. "I hardly think of myself as playing Hamlet, for instance, or Oedipus, or somebody from Noël Coward."

He has moved in the past half-dozen years from his television role in the Western series *Rawhide* to stardom in Italian and American Westerns. In the past four years he has moved to more varied roles, including a Civil War soldier in *The Beguiled,* a disc jockey in *Play Misty for Me*, a soldier in *Kelly's Heroes* and *Where Eagles Dare,* and a big-city cop in *Dirty Harry* and *Magnum Force.* "Any of these roles may be said to be different from my cowboy-bandit image," he says, "but playing them has not been a matter of trying to become a different kind of actor. I played them because they were roles that interested me and that I knew I could handle."

Eastwood's roles have, indeed, ranged from broad comedy in *Two Mules for Sister Sara* to melodrama in *The Beguiled.* In these, and all of his movie roles, Eastwood has displayed another important basis of his broad appeal. He never looks as if he is acting. He has the ability to convince an audience that the actor and the character are the same and that what he is doing is not even acting.

In truth, it is hard in a movie to look as if you are not acting, to appear natural, to make the audience believe that the character on the screen is you and that you are not an actor playing a character. Laurence Olivier, George C. Scott, Rod Steiger, and Marlon Brando are actors whose performance in each film is designed to show their versatility and range. We are supposed to recognize that they are actors and to applaud and appreciate their ability. We never think that Brando, for example, is the Godfather, that the man Brando is like that character.

On the other hand, there are actors who seek the Eastwood impression, that they are not acting at all. Henry Fonda, who has cultivated this style of meshing of character and personality, once told me that the secret was "not to let the wheels show. This is the hardest kind of acting, and it works only if you look as if you are not acting at all."

Eastwood has developed this ability, as did Fonda, John Wayne, and the actor to whom Eastwood is most frequently compared, Gary Cooper. This cool, strong, silent image was not Eastwood's from the start. In almost 250 one-hour segments of the television series *Rawhide,* Eastwood played a brash, hotheaded gunfighter who frequently shot off his mouth and acted emotionally without thinking, a character very much dependent on the father figure of the series. The cool image and the ability to keep the wheels from showing came out of more than two decades of work, and more acting experience than most actors have in a lifetime.

Now Clint Eastwood is number one, and he has been for the past three years. This fact surprises none of his admirers in Japan, where fans have been sending him gifts such as Honda motorcycles since his television days; or in Italy, where he gained his major fame as the Man with No Name in a trio of Westerns. Eastwood's popularity was finally given the reluctant stamp of approval as news in the July 23, 1971, issue of *Life* magazine. Eastwood's face appeared on the cover with the words: "The world's favorite movie star is—no kidding—Clint Eastwood."

Eastwood got there the hard way, and a lot happened to him along the path to success. With most stars, there are stories about their rise and early years, about their battles and accidents. In Eastwood's case, they are generally true.

There is the story of the time he swam three miles from a plane crash at sea, the story about the time he got angry and punched a horse in the nose for kicking him, or the story about the time he walked off a labor job he needed because a friend was fired.

In some ways, the real Eastwood is a living contrast to his screen character. His screen roles usually show him as an emotionally exhausted man who resorts to violence with little prompting. At home, however, he has been known to shoo a fly out of the door rather than deal it a death blow.

He can, indeed, be violent and does have a temper. He has walked off sets and shown impatience with actors or directors. At the same time, he is a protector of animal life in any form, a loving husband to his wife of twenty years, Maggie, and a concerned father to his six-year-old son, Kyle, and two-year-old daughter, Alison.

So Clint Eastwood is not an easy man to understand, but any attempt to do so and deal with his career should start at the beginning.

Clinton Eastwood, Jr., was born in San Francisco, California, on May 31, 1931, but he did not stay there very long. It was the Depression, and Clinton Senior, like millions of Americans, had trouble getting and holding a job. So the senior Clinton, his wife, Ruth, and the baby began to move around from job to job in northern California. They settled briefly in small towns wherever Clint's father could work. During their travels the Eastwoods had another child, a daughter, Jean, and the moving continued.

"I must have gone to ten different schools in the first ten years of my schooling," recalls Clint. And each of the ten years, he grew taller and taller. "We moved so much that I made very few friends. Moving has become a sort of life style for me. Basically, I've been a drifter."

Eventually, Clint's father got a job in Oakland, California, with the Container Corporation of America. In junior high school a teacher convinced Clint to star in a one-act play. Eastwood remembered it as a disaster and thought no more of acting. He entered Oakland Technical High, and while only an average student, was an outstanding athlete, concentrating on swimming and basketball, a sport in which he became a star for the first time. He also worked briefly as a pianist and trumpet player at a bar for meals and beer, but he worked hard at athletics and began to establish a training program that continues to this day. During summers, Clint had jobs around northern California, including hay baling near Yreka, cutting timber and fighting fires for the forestry service near Paradise. Part of his drive and commitment to training can probably be traced to that continuing fear nurtured by memories of his father moving from job to job and the lack of settlement in his early years.

"My father always told me that you don't get anything for nothing," he recalls, "and although I rebelled, I never rebelled against that."

"I was never an extrovert, but I longed for independence, even though I got along great with my parents. I went to work right after I graduated from Oakland Technical High School."

At first, Clint drifted, after his family moved to Seattle. At the age of eighteen, he found himself working in Springfield, Oregon, for the Weyerhaeuser Company in pulp mills and as a lumberjack. He enjoyed this for a year. He then moved to Seattle, where he worked nights at a furnace for the Bethlehem Steel Company. "I wanted to be by myself and earn my own way. Then I went into the army, but I still didn't know what I wanted to do."

After sixteen weeks of basic training, Eastwood was stationed at Fort Ord, California, just a few miles south of San Francisco. His records indicated that he had been a high-school swimmer, so the personnel office assigned him to be the base's swimming instructor. It was during the Korean war, and Eastwood observed that most of the other soldiers were going to Korea.

"How could I protest?" said Eastwood. "I love swimming, and I got to live alone down at the pool. It was a long pool, and most of the guys taking the test couldn't make it, and I'd have to dive in and pull them out."

This swimming ability proved to be more than fun on at least one occasion. Once, after a leave in which he visited his parents, who were then living in Seattle, Eastwood hitched a ride back to Monterey on a navy plane. The plane crashed at sea off Point Reyes, and Eastwood swam the three miles to shore. "I still haven't met the pilot," he recalls. "He had a Mae West, and I didn't. We both made it, but I had the most work to do. I didn't mind the swim, but that five-mile hike before I found a highway really bothered me."

The idea of acting as a possible career first came to Eastwood while he was in the army. Some other soldiers at Fort Ord—Martin Milner, David Janssen, and Norman Bartold—were into acting, and Eastwood was intrigued. (Bartold later appeared in Eastwood's *Breezy*.) Universal-International was shooting some scenes for a film at Fort Ord, and an assistant director pointed out the muscular, handsome swimming instructor. The director called Eastwood over and asked him to read a few lines of dialogue. Before this Eastwood's only contact with acting had been in that junior-high-school play in which he had a few lines; the experience had terrified him.

Eastwood read the lines for the movie director and sufficiently impressed him so that he was invited to look up the director after he finished his army training.

A year later Eastwood got out of the army and promptly arrived at Universal, where he was told that the director was no longer there. But the idea of acting had gotten to him, and he considered going to the University of Washington to study the subject. Instead, he decided to enroll at Los Angeles City College, where he studied business administration under the G.I. bill by day, worked as a gas-station attendant in the afternoons, and as a manager of the apartment house in which he lived at night.

Less than a year later he had a blind date in Berkeley with a pretty blonde model, Maggie Johnson. He married her in 1954 and they are still together some twenty years later. While he continued at school, Maggie worked for an export firm and did bathing-suit modeling for Catalina and Caltex. Although he was not thinking aggressively about acting and not very seriously about business administration, a friend of his from the army, Irving Lasper, a photographer at Universal, urged him to take a screen test.

The screen test, actually an interview on film, was shown around to executives at Universal. Eastwood was offered, and accepted, a stock acting contract at Universal. It was 1954, and the contract gave him a guarantee of forty weeks of pay for a year at seventy-five dollars a week. Eastwood quit school and never returned. For a year and a half he appeared, usually unbilled and without any dialogue, in films starring Rock Hudson and George Nader. Occasionally he would get a line or two of dialogue or get to be an off-camera voice. General-

11

ly, he learned by spending his spare time watching movies being shot.

"They made a lot of cheapies in those days," he recalls. "A lot of B pictures, and I'd always play the young lieutenant or the lab technician who came in and said, 'He went that way,' or 'This happened,' or 'Doctor, here are the X rays,' and he'd say, 'Get lost, kid.' I'd go out, and that would be the end of it."

Two directors at Universal apparently did see potential in Eastwood and gave him somewhat more substantial roles. The directors were Jack Arnold and Arthur Lubin. Arnold, himself a former actor, is known primarily for his fantasy and science-fiction films, such as *It Came from Outer Space* and *Revenge of the Creature*, a 3-D sequel to *The Creature from the Black Lagoon,* in which Eastwood played Jennings, a crew member of the boat that goes after the creature. In Arnold's *Tarantula,* he appeared as an airplane pilot who helps do battle with a giant spider.

Lubin, primarily a comedy director, cast Eastwood as a sailor friend of Donald O'Connor in *Francis in the Navy,* as a costumed Saxon in *Lady Godiva,* and as a ranchhand in *Star in the Dust.*

Although he also appeared briefly in a Jerry Hopper-directed film, *Never Say Goodbye,* starring Rock Hudson, Eastwood felt he was not receiving serious attention at Universal and was ready to say good-bye. He left Universal and went to RKO, where Lubin was doing two pictures, *The First Traveling Saleslady,* starring Ginger Rogers and Carol Channing, and *Escapade in*

*Japan*, with Cameron Mitchell and Teresa Wright.

*The First Traveling Saleslady* gave Eastwood his first substantial role, opposite Carol Channing. His work in the film was sufficient to earn this mention in the *Hollywood Reporter*'s review of the film on June 28, 1955: "Clint Eastwood is very attractive as Miss Channing's beau!" It was a start, but a small one. It is interesting to speculate on the drawing power today of a film which would include the male members of the cast of *The First Traveling Saleslady*. Besides Eastwood, the cast included Brian Keith and James Arness.

In *Escapade in Japan* Eastwood was less fortunate. If you looked away you missed him completely. He played an air-force pilot searching for a downed plane. He has but one brief scene in the film, and two lines, one of which was simply, "Pilot to radar operator."

When Universal refused to raise his salary from $100 to $125 a week, he decided to wait the studio out for six months, at which time they dropped his contract. He wound up in 1957 and 1958 making more money working with a friend digging swimming pools for a contracting company than by acting. During this period Eastwood sometimes was without work for as long as six months. On a digging job one day, one of Eastwood's friends, George Fargo, got into an argument with the boss, who fired him. Eastwood, who needed the money, laid his shovel down and silently turned to join his friend. He is known for such loyalty and for retaining the friends he has made. His closest friends, in fact, are not Hollywood people (though

director Don Siegel is somewhat of an exception),
but friends he made when he was more or less
down and out. Those were the days when he acquired the nickname "Slick," which some of his
buddies continue to use.

The two films in which Eastwood did manage
to get jobs in this period are particularly interesting. In *Lafayette Escadrille,* directed by William
Wellman (whose credits include *The Public
Enemy, The Ox Bow Incident, Wings,* and *The
High and the Mighty*), Eastwood again played a
pilot, the real-life flying hero George Moseley. The
film starred Tab Hunter and was the first truly
major film in which Eastwood appeared. It was also
his first film for Warner Brothers, and his last until
1973, when he returned to do *Dirty Harry.*

Eastwood's other role in this period was as a
former Confederate soldier, now a cowboy, Keith
Williams, in Twentieth Century Fox's *Ambush at
Cimarron Pass,* starring Scott Brady and directed
by Jodie Copelan. Although Eastwood remembers
the film as "a cheap little Western that ... was
even worse than the title," and "a low point of my
movie career," his role was substantial. He was
clearly the second lead in the film and was impressive even if the film was not. In its review of the
film on February 12, 1958, *Variety* stated: "Fine
portrayals also come from Margia Dean, Frank
Gerstle, Clint Eastwood, and Dirk London."

Actually, the role in the film is similar to that
which he developed in the *Rawhide* series. He is a
hotheaded young man, ready to use his guns and
fists. One of the characters describes him as "a
good boy, just young." The primary action in the

14

film stems from Eastwood's antagonism toward the Union Army sergeant with whom he is forced to travel. Eventually, Eastwood and the sergeant, played by Brady, do fight, and in one of the most improbable moments on film, Brady beats Eastwood with a single punch. Eastwood eventually learns to accept Brady as an individual and winds up with him as one of the few survivors of the bloodshed. The role afforded Eastwood an opportunity to display a rather broad range of reactions, and did give him quite a bit of exposure, but it was a minor film that few people saw.

It was the late fifties. Film companies were cancelling contracts and running scared from the threat of television. Eastwood managed to land a few television jobs, including small roles in *Navy Log, Men of Annapolis,* and an episode of Broderick Crawford's *Highway Patrol.* Then he did about a dozen shows in a syndicated series called *West Point,* about cadets at the United States Military Academy. Eastwood had a continuing role in the series as a cadet. "The trouble with that series," he remembers, "was that practically nothing ever happens to West Point cadets in real life. They march, go to classes, play football, study, and go to bed. We'd open an episode with some strong dramatic line like, 'You stole my laundry!' Where do you go from there?"

Many of the early television acting jobs he got were a result of his willingness to do stunts. He was a two-for-one performer, both actor and stunt man, which could save money for a low-budget production. He was especially adept at motorcycle stunts, and motorcycles have continued to be part of his performance in films such as *Coogan's Bluff* and *Magnum Force.*

Throughout his career, in spite of the stunts, he has never had a serious accident, much to the relief of the insurance companies that cover his policy for these tricks.

But back to 1959, with Eastwood out of work.

"I bummed around the industry trying to get a job," he remembers, "and it was the same old story—my voice was too soft, my teeth needed capping, I squinted too much. I was too tall; all that constant tearing down of my ego was bound to turn me into a better person or a complete bastard.

"And I know if I walked into a casting office right now and nobody knew I was Clint Eastwood, I'd get the same old crap. Everything they said was wrong is still there, but now I'm Clint Eastwood and all the other tall guys who squint too much and talk too low are the ones cursing me! It's tough to figure out this town."

One day, with no job in view, and at the age of twenty-eight, he dropped by CBS Television City in Hollywood to say hello to and have a cup of coffee with a friend of his and his wife's, Sonia Chernus, CBS Television story consultant, who is now story editor for Eastwood's Malpaso company. It was a social call, but chance was on his side, and Robert Sparks, CBS Television's executive producer in charge of all filmed programs, spotted him talking to Ms. Chernus and asked if he were an actor. Sparks asked him to follow him down the hall to introduce him to someone wearing battered old clothes.

The someone was Charles Marquis Warren. Warren, a former protégé of F. Scott Fitzgerald, was a successful writer-director specializing in Westerns. He had recently moved to television, where he achieved his greatest success as the creator and executive producer of *Gunsmoke*. Warren was now planning a new Western series, *Rawhide*. He had cast Eric Fleming as the first lead, and now needed the second lead, the character Rowdy Yates, the gunslinging second-in-command. Eastwood read a scene, and a screen test with Fleming was arranged. Warren thought the two worked well together and signed Eastwood as co-star. Ten episodes were shot, but CBS decided not to show the series.

While waiting for the series to be sold, Eastwood landed a role in an episode of *Maverick* with James Garner. It proved to be his only other appearance in a television Western and his last appearance in any television series except for *Rawhide*.

Dejected, Eastwood and his wife headed by train for a visit with his parents, who were again living in Oakland. On the train they received a telegram saying that *Rawhide* was, indeed, going to be used as a series on CBS.

# CHAPTER TWO

# The Rawhide Years, or:
# They Never Reached Sedalia

On January 9, 1959, a Friday night, the one-hour *Rawhide* series debuted on CBS—seven P.M. Central and eight P.M. Standard Time. The blurb in *TV Guide* for the midseason replacement series read:

> Eric Fleming and Clint Eastwood are the stars of a new hour-long Western Series to be seen each week at this time. The stories will revolve around the Western legend of the cattle drive from Texas to Kansas. Frankie Laine sings the *Rawhide* theme music which was written by Dimitri Tiomkin and Ned Washington. This series was produced by Charles Marquis Warren who was producer-director of *Gunsmoke* in its early days on TV.

The series, obviously, tried to capitalize on the Tiomkin song—he had written the *High Noon* song, which popularized the idea of a Western theme sung during a film. It also relied, at first, on Warren's *Gunsmoke* reputation. In fact, the series needed all the help it could get, for 1959 was the season of the Western on television. Competition included *Gunsmoke, Maverick, Cheyenne, Wyatt Earp, Wagon Train, Have Gun Will Travel, Wanted Dead or Alive* (the Steve McQueen series), *Lawman, Rifleman,* and *Cimarron City,* not to mention Sam Peckinpah's excellent but short-lived *Westerner* series, starring Brian Keith. At the time of *Rawhide*'s appearance, there were twenty-nine Westerns on network television, a phenomenon never seen before or since.

Neither Fleming nor Eastwood had any reputation or following when the series began. *Rawhide* was sandwiched between CBS's *Hit Parade* and *The Phil Silvers Show*. Supposedly these shows would help sustain *Rawhide*. Eventually, they both disappeared, while *Rawhide* went on for seven years, with Eastwood in it the whole time. Other network competition in the time slot was stiff. *Ellery Queen* was in color, as was *Walt Disney*.

The gimmick of *Rawhide* was that it would involve a cattle drive in 1866 from Texas to Sedalia, Missouri. The drovers were Confederate veterans.

Charles Marquis Warren's idea for *Rawhide* came from two distinct sources. One was *George C. Duffield's Diary,* an actual diary of a trail boss in the mid-1800's during a difficult trek from San Antonio to Iowa. The other major source was clearly a film, Howard Hawk's 1948 *Red River*. To a great extent, Eric Fleming had the John Wayne role and Eastwood the Montgomery Clift part.

In the course of the next seven years of the series, the cattle never did reach Sedalia, but Eastwood did manage to learn a great deal about acting and to meet a great many directors. He also worked opposite such veteran actors as Dan Duryea, Lon Chaney, Brian Donlevy, George Brent, Victor Jory, Brian Keith, Victor McLaglen, Julie Harris, Cesar Romero, Cloris Leachman, Julie London, Neville Brand, Buddy Ebsen, Peter Lorre, Woody Strode, Kim Hunter, and Robert Culp.

One of the first shows in the series was "Red Wind," written by Dean Riesner. Years later Riesner would write such Eastwood films as *Coogan's Bluff, Dirty Harry,* and *Play Misty for Me.*

In one of the first shows of the series, "Incident of the Shambling Man," Eastwood worked with Academy Award-winner Victor McLaglen. McLaglen, in what proved to be his last role before his death, played a retired bare-knuckle fighter whose daughter-in-law wanted him declared insane. To do so, she provoked a fight between the old man and Rowdy Yates (Eastwood). The show was directed by McLaglen's son Andrew, who went on to do such features as *McLintock* with John Wayne, *Shenandoah* and *Fool's Parade* with James Stewart, and *The Undefeated* with Wayne and Rock Hudson.

As the series continued and Eastwood learned, he kept in shape.

He recalls "working out on Saturday mornings along the Los Angeles River with a friend. We ran as hard as we could for a hundred yards, then walked for a hundred, then trotted for a while, then walked again."

On the set of *Rawhide* between scenes he competed with stunt extras in Indian wrestling and such tricks as holding a sledge upright in one hand at arm's length and letting the head of the sledge back slowly toward his own head. He also did body surfing—using his body as a surfboard— at San Clemente, California.

*TV Guide* called Eastwood "one of TV's finer physical specimens" and asked his advice for staying in shape. He gave it: "Stay away from carbohydrates, especially rich desserts. Keep a scale in your bathroom. Proper rest, not noon to four A.M. Try to be optimistic. Eat fruits and raw vegetables. Take vitamins. Watch the amount of liquids you consume and skip beverages loaded with sugars. Avoid alcohol in excess."

Eastwood followed his own rules and still does. Also, though it is strange considering the cigar-smoking character he developed in Italy, and the cigarette-smoking deputy in *Coogan's Bluff,* Eastwood does not smoke and never has.

A number of the *Rawhide* episodes were directed by Ted Post, whom Eastwood credits with teaching him a great deal about directing and acting. Post was later to be chosen by Eastwood to direct *Hang 'Em High* and *Magnum Force. Hang 'Em High* was Post's first feature film. The white-haired director, who stands about a foot shorter than Eastwood, learned his craft on television films. He did two-hundred episodes of *Peyton Place,* seventy-five of *Gunsmoke,* and dozens of *Rawhide, Medic, Wagon Train,* and *Twilight Zone.*

"The fact that I was nominated for best director on TV for three years in a row doing absolute crap and making it look like ice cream is a big coup for me," says Post. "I'm just now—after all these years of 'paying my dues,' so to speak, and directing shows just to pay the bills—on the verge of getting into areas that I've wanted to be in for a long, long time."

One of the more interestingly directed Eastwood episodes in *Rawhide* was done by Post. A woman remembers accidentally killing her husband, who looked like Rowdy Yates. The killing of the husband is shown, and Eastwood plays the murdered husband. The killing is particularly graphic, with the woman shooting through a door and the door opening to reveal Eastwood shot through the head. It is probably the most striking example of Eastwood on the losing end—even in a dual role—until *The Beguiled*.

Eastwood also got to do a number of comedy episodes on the show, including "Calf Woman" with Julie Harris.

The series moved into the top ten shows in the ratings by 1960, its second year. The next year it was out of the top ten never to return. In Japan, however, it remained the number-one show for years, and Eastwood became a national hero.

The relationship between the Fleming character and the Eastwood character was at the core of the series. Mr. Favor (Fleming) was hard and distant, a very cool character from whom Eastwood clearly borrowed several years later in creating his Man with No Name. As the show progressed, Rowdy emerged as its hero. Toward the end of the run he had assumed unofficial command of attention and the drive. In the last year of the show,

Fleming departed after trouble with the producers, and Eastwood was, officially, the solo star. Fleming later died in a boating accident while on location for a film.

Although the series was successful, Eastwood considered other phases of his career, anticipating the day when *Rawhide* would either reach Sedalia or be forced to leave the air. He considered, briefly, starring in a French farce for a Hollywood little-theater group. "It was just for laughs," he said, but it never really materialized.

In one interview during the *Rawhide* years, Eastwood said: "I'd like maybe to do a feature, something that might get me away from Westerns."

At that time, he had completed eighty shows in the series and did not know he still had years to go. In one episode of the series, he sang a song. A record company heard him and negotiated a contract, but nothing came of it. Somewhere there may exist one of the few records of Eastwood as a singer. Years later he returned to singing briefly, in *Paint Your Wagon*, and a cast album does exist for that. His singing voice can also be heard over the final credits of *The Beguiled*.

He told an interviewer during 1960: "I like to think that *Rawhide* is at least honest. I mean, we're doing stories that pretty much happened." Then he mused, "I wasn't going along anywhere when the show came along. Now I guess I'm a star. I don't figure *Rawhide* will last forever, but I don't figure to walk out on it, either."

So Eastwood continued through one of the best Western series that has ever appeared on television. Its likelihood of reruns is probably hurt most by the fact that the entire series was shot in black and white even after a great many other shows had gone to color.

It the years of the series, Eastwood's character suffered through bouts with malaria, claustrophobia, and various other diseases. He was involved in battles, chased by ghosts, made a fool of by women, and forced to shoot dozens of men. He was constantly involved in fights, and occasionally failed to back away from a fake punch that turned into a real belt. As Rowdy he was thrown from horses and left to die more than once. Like the other characters in the series, Rowdy seldom changed clothes and sometimes forgot to shave.

The elements for the character he would build in his first starring roles in movies were there in the persons of Rowdy and Favor.

As early as 1961, after three years of *Rawhide,* Eastwood was restless. He had a growing belief that CBS had not honored its agreement with him concerning, among other things, his right to appear in other shows or films.

In an interview in *Hollywood Reporter* on July 13, 1961, Eastwood said: "I haven't been allowed to accept a single feature or TV guesting offer since I started the series. Maybe they figure me as the sheepish, nice guy I portray in the series, but even a worm has to turn sometime. Believe me, I'm not bluffing—I've had offers of features in London and Rome that'll bring me more money in a year than the series has given me in three."

CBS knew what they had in Eastwood and quickly called him in to talk things over. After 1961 he was free to appear on other television shows, primarily talk and entertainment shows, and he made it known that he was looking for a feature to be shot during his free months.

With his new power, he also had some leeway to experiment with his own character, Rowdy, which is exactly what he did. His testing ground for many of the characteristics he was to bring to his later screen characters were developed on television. What didn't work was discarded. Some of the *Rawhide* shows turned into disasters, but some of them were among Eastwood's finest moments on film.

Warren, the series creator, who got along well with Eastwood, said of his star when the series was still going strong: "He is more than just a personality, I think. He's an actor. A quite fine actor, in fact. Like any other actor, he beefs now and again, but they're generally justifiable beefs. If he thinks his part is too small in any given script, I'll hear about it."

As part of his greater freedom with *Rawhide*, and his announcement that he was available for features, Eastwood was contacted one spring afternoon in 1964. The contact, a phone call from Italy, was a bit confusing. It seemed that an amalgamated company, Jolly-Constantin-Ocean, was about to make a Western in Spain. They were willing to invest a total of $200,000 in the film, to be directed by a thirty-six-year-old Italian, Sergio Leone, who had done *Colossus of Rhodes* and a few other equally unknown projects.

A number of American actors who were in Europe were contacted to do the role, but they were tied up. Richard Harrison, who had worked with

25

Eastwood and had been one of the actors contacted, was the one who suggested Eastwood.

The offer was a flat $15,000 for six weeks of work. Summer was near, and he had some time off from shooting *Rawhide*. Eastwood agreed, partly to get a free trip to Europe and partly because the role was so different from the clean-cut Rowdy Yates. He went to Italy to shoot *Per un pugno de dollari*. The English title was to be *A Fistful of Dollars*. By the end of the summer he was back in Hollywood assuming that the modest Western he had made would join the other Italian Westerns of the previous few years and be quickly forgotten.

Clint Eastwood is not very often wrong in business, but fortunately for him, he was wrong in this case, and a new episode of his career was about to start.

# CHAPTER THREE

# The Good, the Bad, and the Dollars

Eastwood thought little of the low budget Western he had made. "They couldn't afford an expensive actor," he said, "so they hired me." On talk shows Eastwood would tell a story or two about working with the energetic Leone, but he concentrated on his contract with CBS and another year of *Rawhide* with himself as star.

Word began to creep back to Eastwood gradually that *A Fistful of Dollars* was a hot property. In an interview, Italian director Vittorio De Sica, whose credits include *The Bicycle Thief, Two Women*, and *The Garden of the Finzi-Continis*, called Eastwood "absolutely, the new Gary Cooper." In a visit to the United States actress Sophia Loren asked about Eastwood and found that people didn't know who he was, or they would remember vaguely that he was on some television series. "Well," replied Miss Loren, "he is the biggest star in the Italian cinema."

In Italy, *A Fistful of Dollars* outgrossed both *My Fair Lady* and *Mary Poppins*. Eventually the film earned more than ten million dollars, seven million of it in Europe. But no American release date had been set by the end of 1965. Eastwood continued to shoot *Rawhide* episodes and take in reports about his European success.

From the one film, Eastwood developed a nickname in Italy, "El Cigarillo," for the cigars he smoked as the Man with No Name. In South America he became known as "El Pistolero con los Ojos Verdes"—The Gunman with the Green Eyes.

In its June, 1967 issue, the British Film Institute's *Monthly Film Bulletin* said of the film ". . . it is prolific action which keeps it going, rather than any particular distinction in the direction—or for that matter the acting, though Clint Eastwood is competent as the deadpan hero who sports a stylish poncho and chews an eternally half-smoked cheroot."

*A Fistful of Dollars* was not to be released in the United States until 1967. When it finally was distributed, it met with great popular success, broad television promotion, and critical hostility.

Writing in the *New York World Journal Tribune* on February 2, 1967, Judith Crist, who now writes on film for *TV Guide* and *New York* magazine, said the film was an "ersatz Western" dedicated to proving that "men and women . . . can be gouged, burned, beaten, stomped, and shredded to death." Bosley Crowther in *The New York Times* on that same day also roasted the film but described Eastwood as "a morbid, amusing campy fraud."

According to Eastwood, he accepted the film on the basis of the script and the belief that "if the director had any of the imagination that he seemed to have put down in writing some of the scenes, it would be fun to do." Of the character, he added, "I developed it from what was in the screenplay. A lot of it was taken from the frustration of doing *Rawhide* year in and year out, where I played sort of a conventional hero, nice-guy type. I made the character more—antiheroic—just to be more of a guy who was a gunman out for his own well-being, placed himself first, and didn't get involved in other people's problems unless it was to his benefit."

The film itself was a remake of the very popular Japanese samurai film *Yojimbo* (The Bodyguard), starring Toshiro Mifune and directed by Akira Kurosawa. *Yojimbo* was internationally acclaimed and respected as a brilliant creation of the man who had made such prestigious films as *The Idiot* and *The Lower Depths*. There had been some public response to the violence in the Japanese film, but not a great deal. The violence was generally considered to be an essential part of the theme of the film.

In fact, it could easily be argued that *Yojimbo* is a more bloody and violent film than *A Fistful of Dollars*. As strange as it may sound, all three of the Italian Westerns Eastwood did with Leone are rather bloodless. There are few special effects, and Eastwood's victims fall without the characteristic American spurts of blood common in the late 1960's. In comparison, for example, the death of the villain in *Yojimbo* is long, ghastly, and blood-soaked, while the death of the villain in *A Fistful of Dollars* is flamboyant, with an extreme low shot from the villain's point of view, but no great lingering on the blood.

In the Italian Westerns Eastwood did, there are beatings, but there are really no long lingering scenes of masochism and mayhem. That which apparently offended the reviewers was not the gore but the body count, the apparent indifference to life in the films.

The story of *A Fistful of Dollars* is simple. A rather dirty, cigar-chomping wandering gunfighter (Eastwood) rides into the town of San Miguel and finds two rival families attempting to control the town, the Rojos gang being a little more powerful than the Baxters. The nameless man demonstrates his ability by killing four of the Baxter men and is hired as a gunfighter by the Rojos clan. Ramon Rojos (Gian Maria Volonté) has just massacred an American and Mexican army troop to steal the gold the two troops are exchanging for guns. Knowing that the Baxters will make trouble if they can prove what has happened, the Rojos gang proposes a truce. Eastwood convinces both gangs that there are two survivors from the massacre of the troops. The two sides wanting to get to the survivors—Rojos to kill, Baxter to use them for blackmail—engage in a battle which takes most of both gangs. While all this is going on, Eastwood helps a woman, Marisol (Marianne Koch) to escape with her husband and child. The woman had been kept by force as Ramon's mistress. The Rojos realize what Eastwood has done and beat him, set fire to the Baxter house, and kill the Baxters. The battered Eastwood escapes from his captors and crawls out of town with the help of the town undertaker. After recovering from his beating, Eastwood, wearing a bulletproof vest he has made, faces the five Rojos and kills them all, including Ramon. He then leaves town, supposedly to return the gold to the Mexican government.

During the course of the film, Eastwood, who had been quite talkative as Rowdy Yates, said little, and when he did, it was pointed or comic. At one point in the film he confidently tells a coffin-maker to prepare three coffins as he approaches a gun battle. After the battle, in which he disposes of four men, he puts away his gun and in his low voice says as he walks past the undertaker, "Sorry ... four coffins." By the end of the film, there has been a death toll so high that it is difficult to keep up with it.

There are striking moments in the film for Eastwood. As an actor, he makes the pain of his beating convincing, and as a screen presence he makes his gun battles exciting. The final confrontation, in which he walks out of the mist and down the center of the street, wearing the heavy bulletproof vest, to face the rifle of the central villain is a memorable moment.

There was much more dialogue in the original script than in the final version. "I dropped dialogue," explains Eastwood. "I felt the basic strength of the character—people joke about it now, about how he doesn't talk much—but I felt that you don't dissipate the strength by talking or too much exposition ... I felt that the less people knew about him, the better. It keeps a mystery for the audience. I like to think that the audience acts along with you, that they draw in things. You may get several different things from several different people, but at least that way they're thinking with the film rather than having it thrown at them."

The primary problems of the film are a low budget—the costumes are almost comic in their dude-ness—and some attempt to soften the hard antihero image of Eastwood. Eastwood's saving of the woman who has been taken by the villains and returning her to her husband and son is a rather conventional heroic gesture, not in keeping with his character. Such gestures were to be eliminated in the next films.

Also, there is the distinct impression given in the film that Eastwood is as interested in eliminating the evil families as in getting rich. That, too, would go as Eastwood and Leone developed his character, the Man with No Name.

The antihero is consciously aware of the kind of world in which he finds himself. He is amused—and Eastwood shows this most clearly—and aloof from the grotesque world, the human manifestations of which he destroys like flies, even though he knows it will do no real good: the world spawns evil far faster than he can destroy it. Although the Eastwood character seeks material satisfaction, money, there seems to be nothing in particular he wants to do with it. He is more interested in living according to a certain style, showing others that he knows how to live, how to face danger with amusement and without fear, and if necessary, how to die. In this sense, he becomes an almost mystic survivor, offering a way to face life.

Eastwood's appearance out of the smoke at the end of *A Fistful of Dollars* is designed as a mystical experience to unsettle the killer. Later, Eastwood, in directing his first Western, *High Plains Drifter,* was to take this idea of the mystic antihero to its final conclusion and turn the antihero into a ghostly figure of revenge.

Director Sergio Leone has said: "My first Western, *A Fistful of Dollars,* was the first installment of a triptych. It was born out of a filmic framework· I had seen the Kurosawa film *Yojimbo,* where a theme from the American detective cinema had been transposed into a samurai story. With that perspective, I then proceeded to return the story to its native land by placing it in the context of a Western. . . . While faithful to my own thinking, the film was also inspired by Shakespeare . . . ; the story goes so far as to make of Clint Eastwood the incarnation of the archangel Gabriel. But it was with *For a Few Dollars More* that I for the first time directly grappled with my theme: the friendship that can spring up between two men. Remember, there were—in that film—two generations which opposed one another before uniting."

In the spring of 1965 Leone contacted Eastwood and asked if he would do the sequel to *A Fistful of Dollars, For a Few Dollars More.* Eastwood agreed, and again during his summer break from filming *Rawhide,* went to Spain, where the first film had been shot, and did the second. This time, however, the budget for the film was $600,-000. Eastwood got $50,000 plus a percentage and fringe benefits. He did not know it, but he was on his way to becoming a millionaire.

Of Sergio Leone, Eastwood says: "Sergio, whom I respect very much, would never give me any credit for the style of a film I'd been in with him. This is true even though Sergio and I would hash out ideas together, toss them back and forth. I want to make it clear that I like Sergio, liked working with him. Filmmaking is ensemble work. Leone is a very good film editor, and has a good way of making things important. When you build up to an action scene, it's pow, exciting, and then it's back to being very leisurely. American people are used to shorter films. The European versions of Leone's films are very long. The first time I saw *A Fistful of Dollars*, it was over two hours, absolute mayhem. When it was chopped down, it was better, though the last version I saw was cut too much. Sergio loses objectivity sometimes as far as length of film goes."

In *For a Few Dollars More*, Eastwood again played the nameless man with the cigar who always seems to need a shave. Communication between Leone and Eastwood was improving. Leone began to learn English, and Eastwood picked up some Italian. As in *A Fistful of Dollars* and the subsequent *The Good, the Bad, and the Ugly*, Eastwood's character showed no interest in women and a growing interest in money. In the film, Eastwood is on the trail of El Indio, a mad, drug-addicted killer, again played by Volonté. His reason for pursuit: a big reward for the escaped killer and each member of the gang. Following the gang to El Paso, he encounters another bounty hunter, Colonel Douglas Mortimer (Lee Van Cleef), who gets the better of the nameless man in a hat-shooting incident in the street of the small town where they expect El Indio to rob the local bank. The two bounty hunters decide to become partners. Eastwood joins El Indio's gang, and eventually he and Mortimer track down El Indio, after double-crossing each other several times, and have a three-way shoot-out. Eastwood discovers that Mortimer is not after the money but wants revenge against El Indio, who had killed his sister. Eastwood allows Mortimer his revenge, but, at the end, contentedly piles the many bodies of the gang members on a cart to take in for the reward.

Clearly a relationship of respect develops between the older Van Cleef and Eastwood in the film, though it can hardly be called friendship. No one can actually get to be a friend to the nameless man, the character Eastwood was developing.

This time *Monthly Film Bulletin* (November, 1967) said, "This is the second in this particular series, and is possible even more ostentatiously sadistic than its predecessor. . . . Clint Eastwood as the laconic stranger, he of the chewed cheroot, well-worn poncho, and growth of beard is here joined by Lee Van Cleef. . . . There is no denying that the whole thing is efficiently done."

As in *The Good, the Bad, and the Ugly*, which followed, the final shootout of the film was held in a literal circle, a miniature arena into which Eastwood's character could finally step and prove himself. In both cases, the evil character dies, and although his death is welcome and admirable, it is also upsetting. In *The Good, the Bad, and the*

*Ugly,* Van Cleef, who plays the evil character, tumbles into an open grave, while Volonté in *For a Few Dollars More* is thrown on the wagonload of meaningless dead grotesques. Once dead in an Eastwood film, a character loses meaning. Staying alive is all-important.

While he was in Europe the summer of 1965, Eastwood was asked to appear in an Italian five-part film about witchcraft. He agreed, and De Sica, the director who admired his work, directed him. The seldom-seen film *Le Streghe* (The Witches) features Eastwood opposite Silvana Mangano in modern dress and wearing glasses, a radically different character than the nameless one. The Eastwood segment of the film was called "A Night Like Any Other."

Back home in Los Angeles in the fall of 1965, Eastwood found that Fleming had been dropped as co-star of *Rawhide.* Rowdy Yates suddenly became boss and star. Filming of the series continued into 1966, but with seventeen episodes still to go, *Rawhide* was dropped. Eastwood received a cash settlement of $119,000 and was free and ready to make a third Western in Spain with Leone. This time he would work with both Van Cleef and Eli Wallach, whose credits included such films as *The Misfits, Baby Doll,* and *The Magnificent Seven* and a distinguished stage career.

The shooting schedule was more leisurely, and Eastwood enjoyed working with his co-stars. In his usual terse manner, he says: "I liked working with Eli. It was fun."

Wallach is much more outspoken about Eastwood, Leone and the film.

"Clint," he says, "was very helpful to me. It was my first experience with Italian movies, and Clint guided me through it. It was clear that he knew the Italians and he knew how to make films. He also proved to be more interested in the success of the film than in his own image. When he realized that the focus of the film was going to be my character, Tuco, instead of his character, he came up with ideas and suggestions that made my character even better."

As an actor, Wallach found that "Clint is more a re-actor than an actor. He is like Steve McQueen or Charles Bronson in that. They have great presence and reactions. They can display so much, give the impression of thoughts, feelings, and tensions when we see them react on the screen to another actor."

Wallach also developed great respect for Eastwood as a negotiator.

"I remember," he continued, "that while we were making the picture Clint carried a golf club to practice between scenes. One day we were supposed to do a scene in which a bridge blew up, a big bridge separating the Union and Southern troops. Leone wanted us to be at the edge of the water when the bridge blew. I was new at this and let Clint argue with Leone, who spoke no English. Clint made it clear that we were not going to be near that bridge when it exploded. He is calm and gentle, but he can be very firm. Leone argued, and Clint picked up his golf club and went up a hill with me behind him. He was calmly swinging his club, and I asked him what we were going to do. He answered in his usual quiet voice that we probably wouldn't have to answer the question for a while, since the crew in the confusion would probably blow the bridge up accidentally while we talked. Sure enough, in a few seconds, while Clint was practicing his golf swing, the whole big bridge exploded. It had to be completely rebuilt, and when the scene was shot, Clint and I were a good distance from the explosion."

This time out the Leone film had a $1,200,000 budget and Eastwood received $250,000 and ten percent of the Western Hemisphere profits.

By the completion of *The Good, the Bad, and the Ugly* in 1967, none of the three films he had starred in had yet been released in the United States. Part of the problem was that the Italian company had failed to buy the American rights to the story of *Yojimbo*. By 1967 the Italians and Japanese had worked out a settlement, and the film starring an American and shot in Spain was ready for release in the United States.

*The Good, the Bad, and the Ugly* was by far the most ambitious of the three films with Leone. Each film had improved on the Eastwood image. In *The Good, the Bad, and the Ugly* Eastwood was again the nameless man seeking gold. This time he had a few nicknames given to him by "The Ugly," Wallach, who called him, comically, "Blondie" and "Joe." In the rather complex tale, Wallach and Eastwood are partners in a fantastic scheme whereby Eastwood turns Wallach in for rewards and then rescues him and shares the bounty. One time he fails to share the reward, and Wallach, left for dead, pursues him. They play back and forth with each other while the Civil War rages, until they discover that some gold is hidden in a graveyard. Meanwhile, Van Cleef is also after the gold. Eventually the three meet in the graveyard, Van Cleef is killed, and Eastwood shares the gold with Wallach after first making him believe that he is to be left to hang. Again, a grudging respect between the two men has developed, but it stops short of friendship. Eastwood remains a loner riding off in the distance at the end of the film.

In the Leone films, Eastwood is clearly the "good guy," but what that means in terms of Eastwood's antihero image is radically different from what it has meant in the past. Eastwood is a lawbreaker, a man out for himself. The only thing that seems to move him socially for some reason is a threat to family. Although he pursues money, he remains grubby and is never seen spending it. His indifferent quest for material wealth is striking combined with his lack of interest in sex. It keeps him somewhat removed from the interests of ordinary mortal man. The only thing that ties him to us is his sense of humor; the impression he gives is that he is not taking it all very seriously.

*The Good, the Bad, and the Ugly* contains some of the best moments in the three films. Generally, these moments have no dialogue at all. There is the opening sequence, ending with Wallach in a freeze-frame, chicken leg in hand, flying through a window; Van Cleef's calm murder of a family and the man who hired him for the job; Wallach's confrontation with his priest brother; Wallach and Eastwood's painful dry trek through the desert; a

Civil War battle at a river; Eastwood's loading of his gun behind a door just in time to meet the killers who break in; the graveyard search for the gold; and Wallach's stealing of a gun from a gunsmith.

When the film was finally released in the United States, critic Andrew Sarris, author of *The American Cinema* and contributor to *The New York Times*, wrote in *The Village Voice*, September 26, 1968: "Leone, far from being glossy, seems to revel in the texture of Death Valley dustiness. When Eli Wallach (the Ugly) drags Clint Eastwood (the Good) across a desert, the suffering becomes so intensely vivid and the framing so consciously poetic that the audience is subjected to a kind of Cactus Calvary. No American Western would ever wallow so ecstatically in pain and privation worthy of the most masochistic Messiah. But Clint Eastwood is more a mercenary than a Messiah, and he will be rewarded in this world long before the next. Leone knows this, and Leone's audience knows this. Then why is the mercenary's reward so long deferred? Simply because the sheer duration of the suffering makes Eastwood a plausible lower-class hero whose physical redemption is the contemporary correlative of Christ's spiritual redemption."

Not all critics were willing to compare Eastwood's nameless man with Christ.

*New York Times* critic Vincent Canby called *The Good, the Bad, and the Ugly* "Zane Grey meets the Marquis de Sade," but he admired Eastwood and went on to say, "In those spare, bloody, nihilistic nightmares, photographed in the powdery colors of the Almería desert, Eastwood's fathomless cool was framed with style. The movies required absolutely nothing of him except that he exist, the perfect physical specter haunting a world in which the evil was as commonplace as it was unrelenting."

While he was working on the last of the Leone films Eastwood discovered that one of the small companies, Jolly, which had financed *A Fistful of Dollars* had purchased some *Rawhide* episodes and pieced them together to release as features starring the now-popular Clint Eastwood. The film was actually released as *The Magnificent Stranger*, but Eastwood brought legal pressure and it was withdrawn. In 1967, another small Italian company, Lucas, prepared to release a feature based on two segments of *Rawhide* they had purchased. The Eastwood-starring film was called *El Gringhero*. Again Eastwood protested and this time kept the film from having any release.

Meanwhile, the Leone-Eastwood trilogy made great impact on the box offices of American theaters and established the idea of "a Clint Eastwood movie," just as there were John Wayne movies.

"*Fistful* established the pattern," says Eastwood. "That was the first film in which the protagonist initiated the action—he shot first."

United Artists, which had handled the release of the three films and realized the gold mine it had discovered, began to negotiate with Eastwood to make a film for them, an ersatz spaghetti Western made by Americans and shot in Mexico. Eastwood agreed, and with his films already making money as a triple bill, he went to Mexico to film his first American Western, *Hang 'Em High*. An important memento of the three Italian films was the poncho Eastwood wore. It was the same one in all three, and he never washed it. It now hangs on the wall of a Mexican restaurant in Carmel owned by an Eastwood friend.

Of the Italian pictures, Richard Harmet, of the *Los Angeles Free Press,* wrote: "The Eastwood phenomenon is one of the more interesting things about American movies today. It started off with three Italian films—all directed by Sergio Leone as if the West were one giant opera stage—in which Eastwood played a scruffy, dirty, self-possessed Westerner, who didn't give a damn about anybody, and who was only vaguely on the side of the law.

"There was something about this part that Eastwood played so naturally that almost immediately made him one of our top box-office attractions. On the screen there seemed about him the absolute certainty that he stood above the rest of mankind, and that there was no one he couldn't take with his gun or his fists. Unconcerned about a higher moral order, he shot those who stood in his way.

"Above all, he was in complete control of his environment, certain of his actions and sure there was no obstacle he could not overcome and no human he could not dominate.

"And there is his appeal. Modern man—trampled on by government, beset by pollution, and manipulated by advertising—can only dream of control over his environment, and it is Eastwood who supplies that dream come to screen life.

"Eastwood has been shrewd in his choice of roles. He knows that no matter what the picture, whether it takes place during a modern war or on the plains of the West, his audience expects him to play the Man with No Name, someone who is rough, dirty, and in control."

# CHAPTER FOUR

# Singing in the West

For *Hang 'Em High* Clint Eastwood received $400,000, plus twenty-five percent of the net. Released in 1968, it began showing a profit after ten weeks, with United Artists reporting the fastest payoff of profits in its history. As an example of his popularity, *Hang 'Em High,* in its British second run, beat the first-run box-office records it had established in England. It soon became the top moneymaker in the entire history of United Artists.

Eastwood, who remembers his friends, selected *Rawhide* veteran Ted Post to direct *Hang 'Em High*. It was Post's first feature after many years in Hollywood as a television director.

Eastwood credits three directors with having a major influence on his own work as a director: Leone, Don Siegel, and Ted Post.

Post is clearly a strong Eastwood fan. "I've known Clint since the '50's, when I first directed him in some *Rawhide* episodes, and I always felt he had a certain Gary Cooper flavor. Warm, vulnerable, a dedicated craftsman—those are the elements that make him a star.

"What people don't realize about Clint is he's

also a very fine comedian, and I'm waiting for him to pick a comedy part that will put him on the level of Gary Cooper."

In *Hang 'Em High* Eastwood had an impressive supporting cast, including Inger Stevens, Ed Begley, Pat Hingle, Brue Dern, and Charles Mc-Graw.

In the film, which *Time* magazine in August of 1968 called "the year's grisliest movie so far," Jed Cooper (Eastwood) is hanged by nine vigilantes (headed by Ed Begley) and left for dead.

After being saved by a passerby, Jed is fully exonerated and then appointed deputy by Judge Adam Fenton (Pat Hingle). As Jed rounds up and captures for execution many of the territory's toughest outlaws, he refrains from tracking down his nine hangmen because of the judge's admonitions about taking the law into his own hands. Eventually, however, Cap'n Wilson (Begley), the leader of the lynch mob, shoots Jed to safeguard his own life. Only wounded, however, Jed is nursed back to health by Rachel (Inger Stevens), a young widow who is seeking revenge against the bandits who raped her after shooting down her husband. Once Jed has recovered, he tracks down and kills Wilson's gang, prompting Wilson to hang himself rather than submit to Jed's wrath. Aware that his vengeance has offered him no solace, Jed attempts to turn in his badge, but Judge Fenton convinces him to stay on as marshal.

Eastwood's character was a bit cleaner-looking than in the Leone films, and was to develop a new phase of his screen personality. This time the character had a name, Jed Cooper, and no sense of humor. He was out for vengeance, had decided to take the law coolly into his own hands regardless of the warnings of those around him who try to get through to him.

In its review of the film, *Variety* said: "Eastwood projects a likable image, but the part is only a shade more developed over his Sergio Leone Italoaters [Italian horse operas]."

In his review of the film in *The Village Voice*, Andrew Sarris wrote: "Indeed, strangulation is second only to the six-shooter as a preferred form of homicide in the post-Leone Western. *Hang 'Em High* is concerned ostensibly with the moral ambiguities of a hanging judge ... and his vengeful marshal (Clint Eastwood), himself a lynching victim with a brand on his throat. The script makes gestures toward the transcendental tradition of the Hollywood Western, with references to statehood and law and order, but the transcendentalism is pure rhetoric in this instance. The point of the spectacle is the elaborately staged hangings themselves, vivid and numerous beyond the demands of the debate, catering to the lowest instincts not of lynching hysteria, which is after all a temporary emotional state, but rather of a gruesomely cultivated expertise of spectators who have witnessed too many public executions as if they were Roman circuses."

During the shooting of *Hang 'Em High* in Las Cruces, New Mexico, a scene required Eastwood to be dragged across the Rio Grande River by a horse. The rope was to be around his neck. Although Post wanted a double, Eastwood insisted on doing it himself. Asked why, Eastwood responded, "So I could feel what it was like and what my reaction would be to being dragged across the river at the end of a rope. Then I could play the scene which followed with conviction and feeling."

Two important career events in Clint Eastwood's life took place in 1968. First, he formed his own company, Malpaso. Second, he made his first film with Donald Siegel, *Coogan's Bluff*. Eastwood's relationship with Siegel is sufficiently important to devote an individual chapter to. So for the moment we'll bypass *Coogan's Bluff* and deal with the other films of this period and the establishing of Malpaso.

To get rich, control his scripts and, to a great extent, the films he appears in, Eastwood established Malpaso. He owns the controlling stock in the company but holds no office. By doing this he permits himself to be a product hired out by Malpaso, though he is not under exclusive contract to the company. Eastwood makes no film in which he is not guaranteed a piece off the top of the Italian grosses. He gets salary and percentage deals assuring him upwards of one million dollars per picture, and he frequently spreads the tax bite with arrangements for deferred payments. In most cases, he also gets script control and retains choice of director, writers, and casting.

Recently Eastwood's friend Robert Daley, who oversees Malpaso's production and has been producer on all of the company's films since 1970, described Malpaso's goal as surviving "in a frightening industry by putting all the money on the screen, not in expense-account luxuries or other wasteful practices."

Daley outlined Malpaso's budgetary guidelines:

1. Only accurately and reasonably budgeted screenplays are acquired, and "pre-sold" properties with hefty pricetags are avoided. *Variety* reported that Malpaso had recently turned down a script because it required a railroad and steamships and a possible budget of ten million dollars. "It's too risky to make films today at that price," said Daley.

2. Location shooting is favored over studio work. "There's an esprit de corps that develops on location, and your crews work harder and faster," said Daley, who estimated that only six of Malpaso's two-hundred-plus shooting days in the past four years have involved back-lot or sound-stage filming. The only studio scene in *Dirty Harry*, for example, was the bank robbery, which required a fire hydrant's destruction and careful control of effects.

3. As much as possible, Malpaso tries to maintain an ongoing relationship with key technical people. Malpaso's last nine films have been photographed by either Bruce Surtees or Frank Stanley and edited by Ferris Wester or Carl Pingatore.

4. New technological developments (such as portable camera equipment) are tested and then adopted.

Following establishment of Malpaso and the shooting of *Coogan's Bluff,* Eastwood agreed to appear in *Where Eagles Dare* with Richard Burton. Filmed in Austria in 70mm Superpanavision by

MGM, *Where Eagles Dare,* based on a book by Alistair MacLean, who also wrote *The Guns of Navarone,* was directed by Brian Hutton, a young director who had recently completed *The Pad* and *Sol Madrid.*

During the filming, the Eastwoods' first child, Kyle, was born on May 19, 1968, in Santa Monica. Eastwood was in Yugoslavia at the time, a fact which helped make him negative about distant locations and long schedules. The Eastwoods had waited fourteen years to have their first child. Their second child, a daughter, Alison, was to be born May 23, 1972. Eastwood said at the time of Kyle's birth, "By then Maggie and I knew we could get along well enough to last, that we'd stay together. My wife is very beautiful, and our son, Kyle is—in my opinion, and I am prejudiced—absolutely handsome."

*Where Eagles Dare* dealt with seven men and a woman who are sent by the Allies during World War II into the Bavarian Alps to rescue an American general being held prisoner in a well-guarded castle. Eastwood played an American Army Ranger, Lieutenant Morris Schaffer, who, essentially, backed up Burton, dispatched more than fifty German soldiers, and remained silent. The plot was complex and full of action, and Eastwood had relatively little dialogue, though he displayed a slightly different character, a somewhat naïve assassin who at one point finds himself holding machine guns in both hands and blasting away at advancing Germans.

Under the command of British Major John Smith (Burton), an international commando unit, dressed in Nazi uniforms, parachutes into the Bavarian Alps rescuing a World War II Allied officer from a German castle-fortress known as the Castle of the Eagle. After one of the commandos is found with his neck broken, Smith first rendezvouses with a female agent named Mary Ellison (Mary Ure) and then with another agent, Heidi, who, by posing as a local barmaid, succeeds in getting Mary into the fortress by introducing her as a cousin. Following the murder of a second commando and the capture of three of his other men, Smith and his second-in-command, American Ranger Morris Schaffer (Eastwood), are forced to surrender. But they escape and gain entry into the fortress by crouching on the roof of a cable car. Once there, Smith reveals to Schaffer that the Allied officer is really an actor and that the real purpose of the mission is to discover the identity of German spies in England. After the actor-impostor has been rescued, Smith tricks the three "captured" commandos into exposing themselves as German agents. Now that they have the vital information they were sent for, Smith, Schaffer, Mary, and the impostor must face the problem of escaping. Having wired the fortress as well as certain sites in the village to explode at intervals, they make their way to a cable car. Once aboard, they outwit the Germans, reach the village, leap off the cable car, and, with the enemy still in hot pursuit, make their way through a canal to a garage. There they commandeer a bus and drive to an airfield, where a plane is arriving to take them back to England. Once they are in flight, Major Smith forces one of the mission's organizers, Colonel Turner, into confessing that he is a German agent. To prevent humiliation to Turner and his family, as well as a national scandal, Smith permits Turner to meet a more honorable death by allowing him to leap from the plane.

DeWitt Bodeen in *Focus on Film* called the film "a wildly improbable, tongue-in-cheek action melodrama." *Variety* stated that "Although the film is replete with killings and explosions, they're so integrated into the story that they never appear overdone. It's more of a saga of cool, calculated courage by a couple of heroic types than any glorification of war."

During the filming of *Where Eagles Dare* Eastwood became friendly with both Richard Burton and Elizabeth Taylor. Miss Taylor, in fact, passed on a script to Eastwood for the possibility of their doing it together. Eastwood liked it and sent it to Universal, suggesting that he and Elizabeth Taylor star in *Two Mules for Sister Sara*.

Universal liked the potential box-office success of the team, and Elizabeth Taylor wanted to do it. The original idea was that the film be made in Mexico while Richard Burton was shooting another film on location in Mexico. When the film was ready to shoot, however, with Don Siegel as its director, Elizabeth Taylor, for whom it had been written, was no longer available. Disappointed that Elizabeth Taylor could not make the film, Eastwood wanted Sophia Loren, but that didn't work out, and the role went to Shirley MacLaine.

In both *Hang 'Em High* and *Where Eagles Dare*, his character had become even colder than in the

Leone films. He wanted to do something radically different. The radical difference was to be *Paint Your Wagon*, a musical in which he co-starred with Lee Marvin. For the first time since the *Rawhide* episode almost a decade earlier, Clint Eastwood sang on screen. His two solos proved to be quite good—"I Talk to the Trees" and "I Still See Elisa." In addition, as Pardner he sang three other songs with cast members.

The story, taken from the well-known Broadway musical, involved a woman who marries a prospector (Marvin) and then lives with the prospector and his partner (Eastwood), finally remaining with the partner while the older prospector goes on. There are scenes of action, including the kidnapping of a stagecoach and the collapsing of a town because of tunnels dug under it by the two men, but the Eastwood character is radically different from what it had been previously.

He turns out, essentially, to be a farmer, not an adventurer, and settles down with the woman.

The director of *Paint Your Wagon* was Joshua Logan, whose credits had included the film versions of *South Pacific, Fanny*, and *Camelot*. Logan was certainly not a hard-boiled director, and Eastwood's fans were not enamored of the film.

The box-office receipts were disappointing, but the reviews were good. Part of the problem was the seventeen-million-dollar budget that the film had to overcome. Part of that money was Malpaso's, and Eastwood learned from the experience. He also found that being on location in Baker, Oregon, for five months was not terribly exciting. Most of the time he played golf and worked at a small farm he rented near where the film was shot.

Although Eastwood got along well with Marvin and toured with him on the rounds of talk shows and interviews to promote the film, *Paint Your Wagon* does not appear to be a highlight of his career.

Of the film, *Variety* said: "All the acting is fine, although Marvin tends to become too broad in certain comedy scenes. His dramatic scenes are tops, however, as are Eastwood's and Miss Jean Seberg's."

Vincent Canby, writing in *The New York Times*, claimed that Eastwood sang "in an early Frankie Avalon mode." Ann Guerin of *Show* showed more impatience and said that Eastwood gave the impression in the film that "if only someone would hand him a gun, he could whip . . . the whole soggy film into shape."

To escape the character problems of *Paint Your Wagon*, Eastwood in 1970 returned to action and director Brian Hutton. This time the film was to be a war comedy, *Kelly's Heroes*. Shot in Yugoslavia, the cast included Telly Salavas, Don Rickles, Don Sutherland, Carroll O'Connor, and Gavin McLeod. Although the shooting was plagued by bad luck—sets burning, bad weather—the film was completed and ready for release in 1970.

In the film, Private Kelly (Eastwood) recruits a group of fellow American soldiers to join him in getting to a German-held town in France during World War II. It seems that seventeen million dollars in gold bars is being held there. The idea is that all who join Eastwood will liberate the town and share the wealth.

The group is so successful in their march to the town that the U.S. Army hears of the venture and a general (O'Connor) credits them with the most heroic act of the war.

Eventually, the heroes get the gold after making a deal with the last remaining German tank commander, and they leave the glory to the general.

At one point in the film, Kelly and two others walk alone down the street of a bombed-out town for a showdown with a German tank. The scene is shot as if it were done by Leone, including the characteristic music of the Leone films. Another aspect of the humor comes from Kelly's difficulty in understanding the strange characters he has collected for his caper. Most confusing to him is the anachronistic dropout who keeps talking about "negative vibes."

Ultimately, *Kelly's Heroes* is, in great part thank to Eastwood, a comedy which turns out to be an exciting adventure film at the same time. More important, perhaps, *Kelly's Heroes*, in a strange way, is an impressive antiwar film. The men of Kelly's group are not interested in the war, which does nothing for them and which they cannot understand. It is only when they can see the direct relationship of what they are doing—getting gold—to their actions that they become truly heroic. They have a reason for being heroes and, even, giving their lives, a reason other than the false glory which they cannot accept and which is ridiculed in the general.

Of Eastwood, Hutton has said, "I think we went

Latest U.S. Government
tests of all cigarettes
show True is
lower in both
tar and nicotine
than 98% of all other
cigarettes sold.

Think about it.
Shouldn't your next cigarette be True?

Regular: 11 mg. "tar", 0.7 mg. nicotine,
Menthol: 12 mg. "tar", 0.7 mg. nicotine, av. per cigarette, FTC Report Mar. '74.

Latest U.S. Government
tests of all menthol
cigarettes show
True is lower
in both tar and
nicotine than 98% of
all other menthols sold.

Think about it.
Shouldn't your next cigarette be True?

twenty years of film, from 1947, when Brando hit, until 1967, when Clint hit, with actors who, for the most part, played characters who were confused, not sure of themselves, unable to cope, befuddled. Now Clint is a throwback to the strong, silent men of the 1930's. Clint's character has always been a guy who knows who he is, knows what he wants and goes out and does it. Regardless if he's good or bad, at least he's certain."

One incident took place during the almost six months on location while shooting *Kelly's Heroes* which gives some insight into Eastwood.

During one battle scene in which explosives were used, Don Rickles rose yelling, "I've been shot!"

Director Hutton, dressed all in black, including a black cowboy hat and his own long black hair, assumed it was a typical Rickles rib and said, "Good."

"I want my lawyer," screamed Rickles, according to reporter Ann Guerin of *Show*, who was at the location. "I'm going to sue you, Hutton, for every cent you've got." Rickles began to hop and hobble around while the cast walked over to watch him.

Then, dramatically, Rickles rolled up his pants leg and saw he was not just hurt, but actually bleeding.

"My God," shouted Rickles, overreacting to the scratch, "I *have* been shot."

Almost everyone raced to Rickles' assistance, including the director, cast, and crew. Eastwood was the last one over, walking leisurely.

"Better get Shecky Greene into costume," said

Eastwood without a smile when he joined the frantic gathering.

The cast exploded with laughter, and Rickles gasped, "He doesn't say anything for months, and then when he does open his mouth, he has to be funny. That was vicious, Eastwood." Rickles appealed to the crowd. "Look at him, folks, I ask you to look at him. There he is, Mr. Warmth."

# CHAPTER FIVE

# Coogan and Hogan

*Coogan's Bluff* was the first teaming of Clint Eastwood and Don Siegel and the first film of Malpaso. Things did not go well at the beginning.

"I had made a deal to do my second American film for Universal," Eastwood recalls. "It was a pretty good script, but it was only about three-quarters finished. It really didn't have much of a conclusion to it, but they asked me to do it, and I signed up for it."

"We couldn't find a director at first, and the studio was going to recommend some people, since I had director approval. They recommended everyone but Don. They finally came up with Alex Segal, with whom I met, along with Jennings Lang, Universal's executive producer. Segal had won an emmy for *Death of a Salesman* on television. So I said, O.K., let's see how it goes. But somehow Alex Segal and the writer he was working with got bogged down, and although the writer was good, they just somehow couldn't get it. So I suddenly got a call that there was a big emergency and we had to find another director."

Eastwood began looking at old films, television shows, whatever Universal had. Sometimes he would watch through, other times he would turn off a film after an hour. Then Richard Lyons, a Universal producer and writer, suggested to Eastwood that he set up a meeting with Don Siegel, but Eastwood said no, that he'd rather see something the man had done. "A guy might be great over a cocktail but not coincide with what you think when it came down to working," said Eastwood.

The first thing Eastwood saw of Siegel's was a made-for-television movie, *Stranger on the Run*, starring Henry Fonda and written by Dean Riesner, who had done several *Rawhide* shows.

"I liked it," recalls Eastwood. "I knew he was a guy who knew how to make a film. He wasn't staid or stiff like some of the older directors, and he's not a focus nut like some of the younger television directors, the kind who rack focus back and forth to show that the director is there behind the camera. Then I looked at *The Killers* with Lee Marvin and told the agent I liked Siegel. They told me he was on another project or something but could be pulled off, and I told them to ask Siegel if he was interested in doing the film with me."

Siegel and Eastwood were brought together for a meeting in Jennings Lang's office, and Siegel immediately said that since Eastwood had seen his films, he should see Eastwood's films. Siegel watched the Leone-directed films and liked them. Another meeting was held, and it was agreed that Siegel would work with a writer and prepare a new version of *Coogan's Bluff*.

"I didn't like the new writers' concept at all," says Eastwood. "I thought they were going away from the concept. Meanwhile, the studio had neglected to show either Siegel or me several other versions of *Coogan's Bluff* that other writers had worked on."

Another meeting was called, and Eastwood said he didn't want to do the picture. Siegel, who had directed such films as *Baby Face Nelson, Madigan,* and *Invasion of the Body Snatchers,* got angry, and Lang stepped in, saying, "Will you two simply go somewhere and talk this out and come to some conclusion?"

Siegel and Eastwood went to an office and, as Eastwood recalls, "We immediately started clicking, throwing ideas back and forth. So we decided to make a collage of the best of the other scripts that had been done, bring it to the point where it fell apart, then rewrite it from there."

Dean Riesner was called in, handed the mess of papers, told by Siegel and Eastwood what they wanted, and in two weeks prepared a script both men approved.

The main problem with the character as it had been conceived originally by Siegel, according to Eastwood, was that Coogan was too sympathetic. "He was sort of a hick being taken advantage of by the city," says Eastwood. "I thought that idea had been overdone in the past in Gary Cooper and Jimmy Stewart things like *Mister Smith Goes to Washington,* and *Mister Deeds Goes to Town.* I thought it would be interesting if Coogan looked like a hick, but was actually a hip hick. He's been around a bit, even though he's a small-town guy. Siegel liked that when I got a chance to tell him."

In *Coogan's Bluff,* as finally released, Arizona

Deputy Sheriff Coogan (Eastwood) captures a renegade Indian in the Mojave Desert and, on the way in with the prisoner, makes a brief stop at the home of a woman. The sheriff, played by Tom Tully, finds him in her bathtub and tells Eastwood that he is to go to New York City and bring back another criminal Ringerman (Don Stroud), for trial, since Eastwood had caught Ringerman in the first place. In New York City, Eastwood, still wearing cowboy hat and boots, goes to the police for his prisoner and is told by Lieutenant McElroy (Lee J. Cobb) that Ringerman can't be released yet because he is being treated for a bad drug trip. He says it may be weeks before Ringerman is released. At the station, Eastwood meets social worker Julie (Susan Clark), but decides that though he might like to pursue her, he wants to get back to Arizona. He bluffs his way into the prison hospital and captures Ringerman, who is with his girl friend, Linny Raven (Tisha Sterling). At the heliport with his prisoner, Eastwood is beaten by three men brought by Linny. Ringerman escapes, and McElroy visits the hospital, where Eastwood gets out of bed, steals Linny's address, tracks her down at a crowded discothèque, makes love to her, and gets her to lead him to Ringerman's hideout. But when he gets there, he finds it is a pool hall, where he is ambushed by six men. After a bloody battle, Eastwood goes back to Linny's apartment and threatens to kill her if she doesn't lead him to Ringerman. She takes him to Fort Tryon Park, where Ringerman is hiding, and after a wild motorcycle chase, Ringerman is captured, and Eastwood, after following procedure dictated by McElroy, takes his prisoner to Arizona.

There is some slight modification of the Eastwood character in *Coogan's Bluff*. For one thing, he is very much interested in sex. He also feels a social obligation; at least he accepts responsibility for the escaped prisoner. There is even a hint of an earlier period in the life of Coogan. It had been essential, up to this point, to keep the character backgroundless, possibly to protect his mysterious status and potential superhero quality. The myth would be less than a myth if Eastwood's screen character were a simple human being with understandable human motivations.

Another important difference, partly attributable to Siegel, is that there is actually a change in the character. At the end of the film, although he leaves the social worker, Julie, she apparently has gotten through to him enough so that he displays some human feeling and compassion for his prisoner as he takes him back, a compassion he had been unwilling or unable to show to the Indian at the beginning of the film.

Riesner recalls one confrontation with Eastwood about the script of the film. "I thought," said Riesner, "that it was stupid for Clint, after he finds Linny Raven, to take and bang her, and then believe her when she says she'll take him to Ringerman. He lets her lead him into a trap. He gives her one stiff shot and then she's supposed to be his and tell him the truth. Of course she's going to lead him into a trap. But Clint was right. He made it work in the picture. He has a personal charm that can bring off a scene that would otherwise be distasteful. He knew he could do it, and I didn't. I considered his going with the girl to be an egotistical, blockheaded move, but it worked. Nobody has yet questioned it. Clint has the kind of aura in which he doesn't worry about traps, can walk right into one and know he is going to get out. He gave the feeling that Coogan was a superhero, a guy who can be beaten up, but not vanquished. Clint knew what he could do and carry."

Don Siegel recalled another contribution to the film during the shooting which was characteristic of Eastwood's ability to gauge his own character and what he could do. When Coogan meets the social worker, he follows her outside the police station. The script called for him to joke with a group of children playing and whisk the woman into a cab on the comic pretext that they were escaping from hostile Indians. It was intended to be a comic gesture on his part which takes in the woman. Eastwood thought it was too cute, and Siegel agreed. It came out.

Susan Clark remembers one incident from the shooting of *Coogan's Bluff*. In Julie's apartment, Eastwood is called upon to remove her boots. "They were tight vinyl ones," she remembers. "He tugged and tugged but couldn't get the boot off. They filled the boot with talcum powder and did the scene again. Clint pulled it off and got a face full of powder. His cool was gone. He left the set, enraged, and wouldn't work for the rest of the day. I wouldn't want to be the target of his temper."

The film not only spawned the television series

*McCloud*, with Dennis Weaver in the Eastwood role, but it established an Eastwood-Siegel-Riesner team.

As with many of Eastwood's films, dialogue is limited. There is no dialogue at all for the first forty-five shots (about five minutes) of the film while Eastwood tracks down the Indian. The first line of dialogue then is a smug line spoken by Eastwood as he stands with his gun on the captured Indian. "Put your pants on, chief," says Coogan, and the film begins.

Later, the Eastwood character is evident in an exchange between Coogan and Police Lieutenant McElroy. McElroy is visiting Coogan in the hospital after Coogan has lost his prisoner.

McElroy: Look, Coogan, yesterday we had a prisoner in custody. Today we got a fugitive wandering around with your gun in his pocket. Think about it.

*(This last is spoken slowly and with emphasis. The faint smile leaves Coogan's face. His eyes are locked on McElroy as:)*

Coogan: I have been.

McElroy: We're asking your cooperation. Because what you remember on the plane going home isn't going to help us find Ringerman right now.

Coogan: I'm not going anyplace. Not without my prisoner.

McElroy: Didn't that whack on the skull

63

teach you anything? This is a whole 'nother kind of ball game. You're out of your league. We got twenty-eight thousand cops in this city. You leave Ringerman to us.

COOGAN: It's got kind of personal now . . . .

MCELROY: And a man't got to do what a man's got to do. That it, Wyatt?

COOGAN: That's one way of putting it.

MCELROY: Here's another. Forget it. Understand? Forget it. This isn't just me talking. This comes direct from the district attorney's office. You are not a policeman in the city of New York. Am I getting through?

COOGAN: Still got a badge.

MCELROY: In Arizona you're a deputy sheriff. Here you're just another private citizen with a headache.

*(Coogan's face looks tight and stubborn as he looks at the lieutenant.)*

Most of the dialogue is McElroy's. The Eastwood character knows what he is going to do. He is an individual being told what to do by a man bogged down in the red tape of civilization. For McElroy it is a job to be done. For Coogan it is an issue between two men, a matter of personal honor.

*Coogan's Bluff* is, ultimately, a highly conservative film clearly looking forward to *Dirty Harry*. Eastwood comes to New York to pick up a prisoner. Father figure McElroy tells him to wait. Eastwood, who denies any feeling for others—we had seen him behave without compassion for the Indian he brings in at the start of the film, and we see him treat Julie as a simple sex object—decides not to wait, and he gets his prisoner. He loses the prisoner, and in pursuing Ringerman, he lives through some of the things that have made Ringerman the urban animal he is, just as we had been told reservation living had made the Indian an animal. Eastwood confronts Ringerman's bizarre mother, meets his friends, plunges into the hangouts he frequented, and even goes to bed with his girl. At one point Eastwood tells Julie a story about how he had once been responsible for the death of a prisoner and that the guilt of the experience had caused him to retreat into nonemotion.

In the course of pursuing Ringerman, he begins reluctantly to identify with him. The final confrontation between the two in Fort Tyron Park is an almost affectionate chase. Eastwood catches Ringerman but does not destroy him. Instead he accepts the rules and McElroy's advice. His contact with Ringerman has not destroyed him but caused him to make an emotional move to reject nonemotion and to acknowledge human contact. The change in the Eastwood character is slight, tentative, but it is there. He gives Ringerman a cigarette, which he had refused the Indian, and seems willing to respond to him. The conclusion is clearly with society.

The next film for Eastwood and Siegel was *Two Mules for Sister Sara*, which was shot in Mexico. When Elizabeth Taylor proved to be unavailable, the studio wanted Shirley MacLaine for the role.

"However," says Eastwood, "her casting stretched the imagination a bit and required some rewriting."

In *Two Mules for Sister Sara*, Eastwood, as Hogan, a gun for hire, encounters three men on the Mexican desert who are about to rape Sara (Shirley MacLaine). He calmly shoots the three men and is gathering their belongings when he sees Sara dressing in nun's habit. She enlists his aid, which he grants only because she is a nun, in evading the French soldiers who are following her because she has helped the revolutionaries, the Juaristas. They head across country through various crises, with Sister Sara behaving in a very un-nun-like manner—smoking cigars, swearing, drinking whiskey. For every indiscretion she informs the bewildered Eastwood that special dispensations are granted in such cases. After he is shot with an arrow by a passing party of Indians, Sister Sara gets him drunk and removes the arrow. They then work together to blow up a passing French supply train. They make their way to the revolutionaries, with Eastwood upset by his lust for the nun. In the course of setting up an attack on a French fort, he finds that Sister Sara is a prostitute posing as a nun. Before he has time for anger, he finds himself involved in the attack on the fort, in which his guns and expertise with dynamite assist them in the victory for the Juaristas. The moment the fort is taken, he goes to Sara's room, breaks the door down, and jumps into the tub with her. In the last shot of the picture, she is dressed in gaudy finery riding away in the desert with a disgruntled Eastwood, whose mules are laden with hatboxes.

*Two Mules for Sister Sara* contains the same considerations as other Siegel-Eastwood films, but in spite of its effective violence, the psychological elements are not present. The reason may well be that the film was a comedy and that Eastwood and Siegel never involved themselves in it as a serious statement of feeling. No villain is individualized. The villains are the French, who remain a faceless corporate group. There is no friend, no father. Like *The Beguiled*, which follows it, *Two Mules for Sister Sara* is an exploration of the relationship of men and women and the effect of the relationship on the protagonists, who have somehow come to terms with life and are betrayed by women. Eastwood in both *Two Mules* and *The Beguiled* is the Eastwood at the end of *Coogan's Bluff*. Unlike his earlier films, he is not even discontented with his position and seems to have no internal struggle concerning existence. He and Siegel seem to be saying that even if man somehow finds peace of mind, the psychological acceptance of existence for which he strives and toward which the protagonists of their previous film seemed to be heading, he is still doomed. In a sense, *Two Mules* and *The Beguiled* are considerations of the possibility of survival for the previously unemotional Eastwood character who is willing to enter the world of pain and pleasure.

Eastwood at the end of *Two Mules* is rendered ridiculous, a manipulated and confused pawn of the happy prostitute.

"Clint," says Siegel, "has as absolute fixation as

an antihero. It's his credo in life and in all the films he's done so far. And it has been very successful, certainly for Clint and for those who own a piece of his pictures. He insists on being an antihero. I've never worked with an actor who was less conscious of his good image."

The film consciously tried to capitalize on Eastwood's Man-with-No-Name image, including the musical score by Ennio Morricone, who had done the Leone films. Again he was the unshaven gunman in Mexico, but this time he was not as much in control; he was being controlled by a woman.

An alert viewer will note in the film that Eastwood, who is ambidextrous, uses both hands in fighting, shooting, and throwing dynamite. Every bit of his athletic ability was called upon by Siegel for the fight scenes and the attack on the fort.

At one point while on location in Durango, Siegel looked up while preparing a shot to see Eastwood's horse kick the star. Instantly Eastwood punched the horse right in the mouth and walked off limping and holding his now-sore hand.

When asked about the film, Eastwood recalls the scene in which he gets drunk so that Shirley MacLaine, with whom he very much enjoyed working, can remove an arrow from his shoulder. "That," he says, "was the best scene I've ever played. Some critic in a small town told me once that he didn't like that scene, and I said, 'Well, you'd better give up on me, then, because that's the best I can give out.' A lot of people don't appreciate the values of playing drunkenness. Drunkenness is probably the most abused condition of a human being to be acted out. Everybody always plays the result of drunkenness so badly.

"One thing I like to do is not rehearse. I like to rehearse the geography of a scene, mechanically, and how it's going to work, and then just do it. That's how we did that scene. Don Siegel for one has gotten used to this. I did the same thing later in *Play Misty for Me*, because Jessica Walter liked to work that way. A million times I've done scenes in which the best take is left off the film. Something fantastic happens, like an improvisation, and then all of a sudden you don't have it anymore."

Eastwood's respect for living creatures was evident during the filming on location in Mexico. In the United States animals are protected by the Society for Prevention of Cruelty to Animals, and a member of SPCA is on hand when any film is shot using animals. No such restrictions apply in Mexico. When the script called for Eastwood to kill a rattlesnake, he refused on principle, but finally relented.

The reviews of *Two Mules for Sister Sara* were generally favorable. *Entertainment World* on April 17, 1970, observed: "As Hogan, Clint Eastwood shows that he not only possesses a strong screen personality, but he can also deliver a line with fine comic flair. Moving and talking at his own easy-going pace, he is charming and the perfect he-man hero."

Andrew Sarris in *The Village Voice* on July 9, 1970, observed: "Eastwood and MacLaine are extraordinarily good at evoking the old Eden of Hollywood movies in which the magic of romanticism was actually enhanced by the meanness of repression."

During the shooting of the film, nearly everyone but Eastwood came down with either the flu or dysentery. Eastwood, recalls Siegel, continued to exercise and eat fruit. Brian Hutton also remembered that during the shooting of *Kelly's Heroes* injuries were frequent, but nothing ever happened to Eastwood.

At one point in the filming, production had to wait for Miss MacLaine to recover. When she did, she was anxious to finish the film and get out of Mexico. It had been a far cry from her last film, *Sweet Charity*.

The exchanges between MacLaine and Eastwood show a further development of the cynical antihero that Eastwood had created. In the case of *Two Mules*, the exchanges were comical, but nonetheless serious, like this exchange between the two.

SARA: So you are not married?

HOGAN: Nope.

SARA: Ever been?

HOGAN: Nope.

SARA: Would you like to be?

HOGAN: Frankly, no.

SARA: But don't you want a woman of your own?

HOGAN: What for?

SARA: To share your name, to be your companion, to bear your children?

HOGAN? . . . to tell me to stop drinking, to nag me about gambling, to beg me to save my

money, to whine about her aches and pains . . .
no, thank you, ma'am.

SARA: What a lonely life.

HOGAN: What a great life. Women, when I
want them, and none with the name of
Hogan.

By 1971, Eastwood's films had grossed an estimated $200 million, and he was commanding a
fee of about one million dollars, plus a percentage
of the gross of each film he contracted to make.
Producers were anxious to take him up on the offer and considered it a bargain.

But Siegel and Eastwood had an idea for a
change for both of them. In *Two Mules for Sister
Sara,* Eastwood had been the victim of one woman
in a comedy. Why not make him the victim of a
houseful of women and do it as a tragedy?

# CHAPTER SIX

# Gulliver in the Lair of Sparrows

"Maybe a lot of people just don't want to see Clint Eastwood's leg cut off." Those were the phophetic words of Jennings Lang, Universal Studios' vice-president in charge of feature films.

"It was great," said Lang later, "but no one went to see the picture. And I will have great pause the next time I get a script that would put a heroic image like Clint Eastwood in a position like that."

The film was *The Beguiled,* directed by Siegel and starring Eastwood. It was the only Eastwood film which did not do well in the United States. Part of the reason, indeed, may have been that Eastwood in the film not only loses his leg, but is murdered by a houseful of women. It was a far cry from the Eastwood image of invincibility of the past. The Eastwood character might be beaten, dirty, and bloody, but he was always confident and in control, and the audience knew he would triumph. *The Beguiled* was another story.

The film received rave reviews in Europe and did, indeed, make money. It was only Americans who preferred not to see such things happen to the Man with No Name.

In *The Beguiled*, Johnny McBurney (Eastwood) is a Union soldier wounded behind Southern lines in the Civil War. He is found by a small girl (Pamelyn Ferdin), who brings him back to a school for girls run by Martha (Geraldine Page), assisted by Edwina (Elizabeth Hartman) and a slave (Mae Mercer). Martha reluctantly takes him in, and fearing he might die on the way to prison, decides not to turn him in to a passing Southern patrol. Eastwood recovers slowly and works hard at charming the school's women and six female students. He succeeds, hoping to escape when his leg recovers enough for him to walk without crutches. When a band of Southern soldiers almost captures him, he is protected with lies by the women. One night, as he stands in the hall, deciding whether he should go to the bedroom of Martha or Edwina, he is found by one of the students, Carol (Jo Ann Harris), who convinces him to come to her room. The noise they make in bed awakens Edwina, who, finding Eastwood in the girl's bed, becomes hysterical and pushes him down a stairway.

His leg badly broken, he is carried semi-conscious into the dining room, where Martha vindictively amputates his broken leg, claiming it is for the sake of his health. When he awakens to find his leg gone, his anger becomes uncontrollable. He humiliates Martha before the girls by revealing that she had an affair with her brother. He announces either he will stay and have his pick of the women or he will turn them in to the now-advancing Union soldiers. In spite of Martha's attempt to stop her, Edwina sympathetically goes to join him in his room.

That night Eastwood is invited down for dinner and apologizes for his behavior, saying that he plans to marry Edwina. However, Martha confesses that they have fed him poison mushrooms. He rises, staggers out, and collapses, to die in the hall while the women finish their meal. The picture ends as they carry his body out of the school gates to be buried.

"Universal owned the property," explains Eastwood, "and I was intrigued by it. It's a wild, wild story. When we were working in Mexico on *Two Mules for Sister Sara,* I came up to Los Angeles for a week while Don was shooting around me. They gave me the story at that time, and I read it and liked it. Then I told Don about this strange thing I had read. I said it was the type of thing that could really be something exciting. It probably wouldn't make any money, but on the other hand, it might go right through the roof or right down the toilet. Well, Don was wrapped up with *Sister Sara,* and it was hard to get him to read anything new. He finally read it and said, 'Gee, that is interesting,' and he started getting excited about it, and I started having doubts. Then he became the leading force and helped me decide. He said, 'You can always do the kind of role you're known for, but you may never again get a chance to do this type of film.'

"So I said, 'Yes, you're right, let's give it a try.' "

Vincent Canby in *The New York Times,* April 11, 1971, said of the film that people "will be hard put to accept it, other than as a sensational, misogynistic nightmare. But I must say I found it interesting (even when it approached the ludicrous) because of its place in relation to other Siegel films and because I have nothing but appreciation for the performers, especially Geraldine Page, Elizabeth Hartman, and Mr. Eastwood."

Many of the American reviewers were less kind, but the European reviews made up for it.

Francois Nourissier in *L'Express* (Paris), August 16–22, 1971, said, "Often, the film has, almost, the makings of a great masterpiece." He went on to say that Eastwood was excellent as McBurney.

Albert Cervoni in *La Vie Culturelle* wrote, "The violence of the war, a violence always present in the film but through echoes (at once sharp and dully deafening), and a violent yet restrained sexuality constitute the raw materials of this major film that is further distinguished by exemplary balance and a remarkable cinematic direction with an extreme concern for faithful recreation of the climate of the epoch."

The film was made with locations in New Orleans. Publicity before the film's release was forceful and sometimes bizarre. For example, at one point it was considered that Pistol Pete Maravich, the former Louisiana State University basketball star who is now a National Basketball Association superstar with the Atlanta Hawks, was going to have a role in the film. It turned out that he was going to have a walk-on for which he would be paid $22.50, but even that did not materialize. Consideration was also given to casting Jeanne Moreau or Anne Bancroft in the lead with Eastwood. Over one hundred teen-agers were tested for roles as the girls. One fourteen-year-old came to Los Angeles from New Orleans on the chance of getting a screen test.

Throughout, both Siegel and Eastwood were confident that they were making an important film, and Siegel's confidence in Eastwood was reinforced.

"From the beginning of our relationship," says Siegel, "I found Clint very knowledgeable about making pictures, very good at knowing what to do with the camera. I also found that he is inclined to underestimate his range as an actor. I think he is a very underrated actor, partly because he is so successful. We started out with a cautious mutual admiration. He started to come up with ideas for camera setups. I started to call these Clintus shots, and even if I decided not to use them, they invariably gave me another idea, threw me into a Siegel-ini shot. We've developed this, and it has become fun making pictures with him.

"We don't try to win points with each other. He doesn't try to impress on me that he is a big star, and I don't try to impress on him that I'm a big director. If either one of us is really steadfast in an argument, whatever it is, the other has enough respect to realize that there is something to it and give in.

"Clint is a very strong individual, on and off the screen. He doesn't require, and I don't give him, too much direction. A good rule with Clint is that when you give him a direction, be sure you're right about it. If you don't think you're right, don't say it.

"Clint knows what he's doing when he acts and

when he picks material. That's why he's the number-one box-office star in the world. His character is usually bigger than life. In spite of the current mode, I think people don't really want to see pictures about mundane things and ordinary people. Clint's character is far from mundane or ordinary. He is a tarnished superhero, actually an antihero. You can poke at a character like that. He makes mistakes, does things in questionable taste, is vulnerable. He's not a white knight rescuing the girl; he seduces her."

On occasion, Eastwood has shown signs of temper when cast or crew fail to live up to the kind of professionalism he expects. On the other hand, he can be gentle and helpful when he is convinced that the individual is trying and capable of delivering.

Elizabeth Hartman, whose credits include such diverse films as *You're a Big Boy Now*, *A Patch of Blue* (for which she received an Academy Award nomination), and *Walking Tall*, played opposite Eastwood in *The Beguiled*. She had not done a film in some time when the role of Edwina came to her. She was scared and felt particularly alone on location in New Orleans. Much of the credit for her fine performance she attributes to Eastwood, who, she says, showed great patience and understanding in addition to a fine sense of humor.

"We took a chance on that film," says Eastwood, "because it certainly wasn't a highly commercial film. It could have been. Like any film, you never know what's going to hit the public's fancy. We figured it could be a very good film, and that was

77

important. I thought it was a very exciting film. Whether it's appealing to large masses or not, I don't know, but execution-wise, I thought it was very well done."

Since its initial unsuccessful release, *The Beguiled* has developed an underground reputation and has begun making money. Both Eastwood and Siegel realized that this might happen, and indeed, had wanted the film promoted in quite a different way from the other Eastwood films.

However, on its release, the studio chose to handle the film as if it were an Eastwood action film. The results were disastrous, and Eastwood feels the promotion of the film was all wrong. He would have preferred a small opening for the film, an opportunity for it to receive a reputation as an art film.

In fact, the picture was chosen as the first official entry for the USA Film Festival in Dallas in 1971. The film had also been invited to be in the prestigious Cannes Film Festival, but since it had already opened for a commercial screening in Milan, Italy, the committee ruled that it was not eligible.

The film may have had a mixed critical response and an uneven public reaction, but Eastwood's position as a star remained secure and profitable. For *The Beguiled*, for example, he worked a little more than ten weeks at a salary of $60,000 a week, which came to over half a million dollars. Siegel, with a smile, remarked, "That is better than a stick in the eye."

The next step for Siegel and Eastwood was to get back that critical audience, the public, with their next effort, and they did more than that with *Dirty Harry*.

At the same time, Eastwood was more and more determined to become involved with directing. He resolved to do two things: act in films making use of the screen image he had developed so carefully, and direct films that were interesting to him.

Eastwood had directed several scenes in his films with Siegel, and in fact directed a short promotional film about Siegel and *The Beguiled*, which was shown on network television.

The film featured Eastwood talking about Siegel and explaining a bit about how films are shot. Having done it, he felt ready for a major effort. So, using Malpaso funds, he did *Play Misty for Me*.

# CHAPTER SEVEN

# Eastwood on Eastwood

Clint Eastwood moves quickly. I had been at Universal Studios, where Eastwood's Malpaso Production Company is headquartered, for three weeks before I could catch up with him. A few nights before I made my third try to catch him at his Universal bungalow, I had seen a preview of *Play Misty for Me*, Eastwood's first attempt at directing.

I got through to Eastwood's producer and associate Bob Daley, who called across to Eastwood and asked if he could squeeze me in before he got in his Sting Ray and headed back to Carmel, where he lives. The interview was set for six-thirty that night.

Eastwood's name is not on Bungalow 64, which is about thirty yards from his friend Siegel's bungalow. The outer office is covered with pictures of Eastwood from his movies and a large Eastwood poster showing him in a Sergio Leone picture. There is also a picture of Don Siegel in his role as a bartender in *Misty*.

Eastwood, wearing a blue pullover T-shirt, greeted me by name, and we went into his office.

He is a nonslouching six-foot-four, as soft-spoken in life as in his movie roles.

His office is large—comfortable executive conference table at one end, sofa against one wall, large desk across the carpeted room. On the wall above the sofa was a huge poster in Italian for *Where Eagles Dare*. Another wall contained a slashed portrait of Eastwood, which figures in the plot of *Misty*.

Popular disc jockey Dave Garland (Eastwood) finds himself at loose ends when his girl friend, Tobie Williams (Donna Mills), unexpectedly leaves town. One night, while drinking at his favorite bar, Eastwood meets Evelyn Draper (Jessica Walter), an attractive brunette who suggests a visit to her apartment and then informs him that she is the girl who regularly phones his radio station to request that he play the song "Misty." By morning, however, it becomes apparent to Eastwood that what he thought was a one-night stand is really a romantic obsession on Evelyn's part; openly pursuing him, she begins dropping in at his home uninvited, at one point disrupting him while he and his co-worker Al Monte are preparing a presentation for station owner Madge Brenner. Further, when Tobie returns and Eastwood resumes their relationship, Evelyn becomes uncontrollably jealous, spying on them during their romantic walks and even cutting her wrists in a desperate effort to win Eastwood's attention and concern. After entrusting Evelyn to the care of Frank Dewan, a doctor friend, Eastwood leaves to discuss a job offer with Madge; but Evelyn interrupts their luncheon and so hysterically insults the older woman that the deal is permanently squelched. Arriving back home, Eastwood finds his cleaning woman, Birdie, almost slashed to death with a razor, his apartment wrecked, and a dazed Evelyn being questioned by Police Sergeant McCallum. With Evelyn removed to a sanitarium, Eastwood sees Tobie again and learns that she has taken a new roommate named Annabelle. But before long, Evelyn phones Dave at the station to tell him that she is cured and on her way to Hawaii—and would he please play "Misty" for her? Then late that night, awakened by the sound of "Misty" coming from his stereo, Eastwood finds Evelyn standing at the foot of his bed. Suddenly lunging, she makes an unsuccessful knife attack and then runs off. A few days later, Eastwood recalls that Evelyn once quoted two lines from Poe's "Annabelle Lee" to him over the phone; remembering that Tobie's new roommate is named Annabelle, Eastwood calls McCullum and asks him to rush to Tobie's apartment. When Eastwood gets there, McCallum is lying dead with a pair of scissors in his chest, Tobie is bound and gagged on the bed, and the deranged Evelyn is once more poised with a knife. In staving off her violent attack, Eastwood hurls Evelyn across the terrace, and stumbling backward, she falls off the edge, plummeting to her death on the jagged rocks below. As Eastwood unties Tobie and helps her from the apartment, "Misty" once more begins to play on the radio.

With darkness coming over the San Fernando mountains beyond the bungalow, the actor and, now, director sat and talked for a few hours over a couple of beers.

KAMINSKY: You've done four pictures with Don Siegel as your director. He appears as an actor, the only time he has done so, in the first movie you directed, *Play Misty for Me*. The only other thing you have directed is a short, the subject of which was Don Siegel. What is there about the man that you obviously like so much?

EASTWOOD: It's a mutual-admiration thing. He likes a lot of my ideas, and I like his. I like his attack on directing. He's very straightforward. His films always have energy. He has that energy as a person. He moves briskly and tries to get right to the point in directing. I've been involved with some directors who are wishy-washy, don't know what they want. Don never starts rolling until he has an attack. We change a lot of things in the middle, but even the changes are positive, forward. I think that's what I like: his forward momentum is always there. He never gets bogged down, even in disaster. I think he's fantastic. We have worked a lot together, and probably will in the future. I feel he is an enormously talented guy who has been deprived of the notoriety he probably should have had much earlier because Hollywood was going through a stage where the awards went to the big pictures and the guys who knew how to spend a lot of money. As a result, guys who got a lot of pictures with a lot of effort and a little money weren't glorified. So Don had to wait many years until he could get to do films with fairly good budgets. He's the kind of director there's not enough of. If things don't go as planned, he doesn't sit down and cry and consider everything lost, as some directors do.

KAMINSKY: How does working with Siegel compare to working with Sergio Leone.

EASTWOOD: Don likes to hear ideas. He has an ego like everyone else, but if a janitor comes up with something, he won't turn it down. He'll take from anybody. He kind of breeds an atmosphere of participation. Sergio Leone, whom I respect very much, would never give me any credit for the style of a film I'd been in with him. Don would and does. This is true even though Sergio and I would hash out ideas together, toss them back and forth. I want to make it clear that I like Sergio, liked working with him. Filmmaking is ensemble work. A director who can have a clear focus in a film, a clear idea of the style he's moving toward, and still draw creative things out of everybody working with him has an atmosphere which will make superior movies in the long run. The director is still the leading force, the captain.

KAMINSKY: Did your outlook change when you became a director? Do you appreciate the problems of a director more now, after *Misty*?

EASTWOOD: No, I knew what I was getting into. I've been in front of a camera for a lot of hours in the last eighteen years. In TV, I saw so much that I *wouldn't* do as a director. I felt prepared.

KAMINSKY: In *Misty*, I know the first scene you did was the one in which Don Siegel had his acting debut. Did you do that purposely to put him on a spot?

EASTWOOD: Actually, it just worked out that way. I

tell everybody I did it that way because it was my first day on the set, and I wanted somebody to be more nervous than I was, but actually I just started with that sequence because I wanted to start with something moderate, not too rough. We had three days scheduled for it, since it was Don's first acting job, but we did it in a little over a day. He was very nervous during the first few takes, but by the second morning he was an old pro.

KAMINSKY: When you work as a director, do you feel you're working the way he does, or some other director, or what?

EASTWOOD: No, I work my own way, although I've certainly been influenced by the directors I've worked with over the years. Siegel has had influence on my directing, but so has Sergio, and so has Ted Post [*Hang 'Em High*]. And so have other guys from the television years, as well as directors whose work I've seen though I've never met them.

KAMINSKY: What other directors do you admire?

EASTWOOD: Well, I used to love Hitchcock, some of that earlier stuff.

KAMINSKY: Why did you decide to do *The Beguiled*, which was so different from everything you'd done earlier?

EASTWOOD: The studio owned the property, and I was intrigued by it. It's a wild story. I told Don about it and told him I thought it was the kind of thing that could go right to the roof—or right down the toilet. He eventually read it and liked it, and then I had doubts. He was kind of the leading force in getting me to do it, as it

85

wound up. He said: You can always be in a Western or adventure, but you may never get a chance to do this type film again. The studio wanted to do it, so we did it.

KAMINSKY: Did you think you were taking a chance because it was different from what you had been doing?

EASTWOOD: Only in the sense that it wasn't a typical commercial film, but we thought it could be a very good film, and that was important.

KAMINSKY: How would you compare it with the other ones you've done?

EASTWOOD: I think it was a very well-executed film, the best-directed film Don's ever done, a very exciting film. Whether it's appealing to large masses or not, I don't know.

KAMINSKY: How did you come to do *Two Mules for Sister Sara?*

EASTWOOD: I had read the script, which was given to me by Elizabeth Taylor when I was doing *Where Eagles Dare* with her husband. We wanted to do it together, and the studio approved of the combination, but she was going through some deal where she didn't want to work unless it coincided with Richard's working, so we had it set up to do in Mexico while Richard was working there on something else, but then there were some other problems, and I think the studio kind of leaned toward Shirley MacLaine, because they had such high hopes for *Sweet Charity* at that time. It required some writing, and the casting of Shirley stretched the imagination a bit. It would have been ideal for Sophia Loren.

One of Clint Eastwood's earliest film appearances was in FRAN-CIS IN THE NAVY (1955). Above, with Phil Garris, Richard Erdman and Martin Milner in a publicity shot. Below, with Donald O'Connor.

*Eastwood appeared with Ginger Rogers and Carol Channing in THE FIRST TRAVELING SALESLADY (1956). Above, with David Brian, Frank Wilcox, Dan White, Barry Nelson, Carol, and Ginger (behind bars).*

*That's Clint behind Tab Hunter's hat in LAFAYETTE ES-CADRILLE (1958). The man with the baton is Marcel Dalio.*

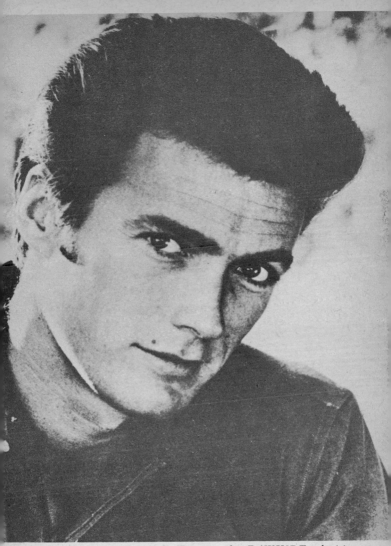

*Clint Eastwood as Rowdy Yates in the RAWHIDE television series (1959).*

*Clint Eastwood makes his first appearance as The Man With No Name in A FISTFUL OF DOLLARS (1964).*

*Colonel Mortimer (Lee Van Cleef) offers a deal to "El Cigarillo" (Eastwood) in FOR A FEW DOLLARS MORE (1965).*

Tuco, The Ugly (Eli Wallach), gets the drop on "Blondie" in in THE GOOD, THE BAD AND THE UGLY (1966).

The Bad (Lee Van Cleef) has the drop on the anguished Ugly (Eli Wallach) and the nonchalant Good (Clint Eastwood).

*A clean-shaven Eastwood as Jed in HANG 'EM HIGH is nursed back to health by Inger Stevens (1968).*

*Don Siegel suggests a movement to Clint and Susan Clark during the shooting of COOGAN'S BLUFF (1969).*

*Eastwood made his singing debut in the musical, PAINT YOUR WAGON (1969).*

*With co-stars Jean Seberg and Lee Marvin in PAINT YOUR WAGON.*

*Eastwood appeared with Richard Burton and Mary Ure in WHERE EAGLES DARE (1969).*

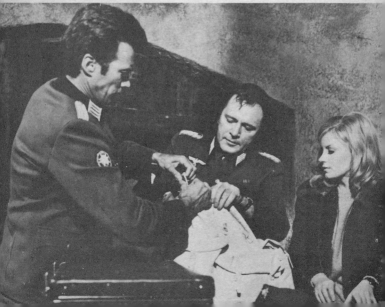

*Kelly (Clint Eastwood) and "Crapgame" (Don Rickles) in*
*KELLY'S HEROES (1970).*

*On location for*
*KELLY'S HEROES*
*in Yugoslavia.*

In *TWO MULES FOR SISTER SARA* (1970), Clint returned to his cigar-chomping, grubby image.

*Hogan (Clint) and Sara (Shirley McLaine) break between scenes for* TWO MULES FOR SISTER SARA *while on location in Mexico.*

In *THE BEGUILED (1971)*, McB (Eastwood) found himself the victim of a houseful of predatory females led by Geraldine Page.

Cameraman Bruce Surtees, actor Eastwood and director Siegel set up a scene for *DIRTY HARRY (1971)*.

*In DIRTY HARRY, Clint did his own stunts, including this leap onto a moving bus.*

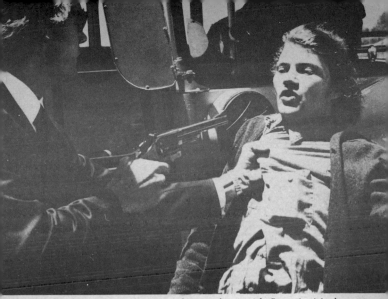

*Harry and his Magnum come face-to-face with Scorpio (Andy Robinson) in DIRTY HARRY.*

*Eastwood relaxes between takes with son Kyle.*

The clinging Evelyn (Jessica Walter) clutches at the bewildered Dave in PLAY MISTY FOR ME (1971).

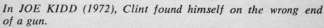

In *JOE KIDD* (1972), Clint found himself on the wrong end of a gun.

In HIGH PLAINS DRIFTER (1972), Eastwood doubled as star and director. Above, in action for a scene. Below, The Man With No Name again roamed the West, this time with a small sidekick, Billy Curtis.

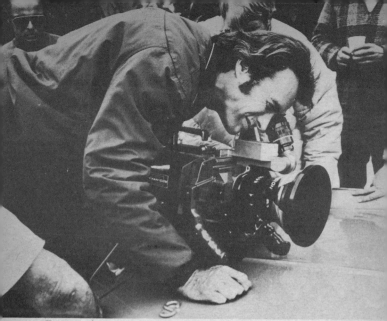

Eastwood gets a camera-eye view of a scene to be photographed inside an automobile for BREEZY (1973), which he directed but did not appear in.

With MAGNUM FORCE (1973), Eastwood returned to the character portrayed in DIRTY HARRY, with much success.

KAMINSKY: Would you comment on the different styles of Leone and Siegel?

EASTWOOD: Leone is a very good film editor, and has a good way of making things important. When you build up to an action scene, it's pow! exciting, and then it's back to being very leisurely. Don is a little more impatient. American people are used to shorter films. Don is more direct, though *The Beguiled* was a little more leisurely. It was very smooth; everything sort of folded over nicely.

KAMINSKY: Do you feel that about particular sequences or the whole film?

EASTWOOD: The whole film, because it was different. Don usually does those detective-type films. *Dirty Harry* will need Don's kind of energy; it will be very important to that film. I don't think it will be the most exciting I've ever been in, but I do have good feelings about it.

KAMINSKY: *Dirty Harry* has so little dialogue.

EASTWOOD: It's a very physical-moving film. I'm anxious to see the first cut. Don usually makes the first cut and then we run it together and sit and play around with it, and then after he's picked any ideas he has off me, we kick it around, try it and see how it looks, and then tell the studio that's it.

KAMINSKY: Let's talk about *Play Misty for Me* now. First, why did you stick with the particular song "Misty," since you had so much trouble getting it?

EASTWOOD: The problem with a new song would have been that you had to play it a lot in the film, and the way the script was designed, you couldn't play the song a lot. I couldn't use it as an underscore. The script was designed by Bob Daley and myself to have most of the music from a source. Now, I needed a song that was not so old that the present generation would say: Gee, I never heard of that. It had to be an old-new song, something that everyone from eighteen on would recognize. The studio wanted me to use "Strangers in the Night," which they own, but it's not a classic, though it was a hit, and there's that dooby-dooby-do at the end. I just thought it wouldn't work. Also, it had already been used once in a movie, and I just didn't like the title "Strangers in the Night" for the movie. It was a square hit song, you know.

KAMINSKY: Your relationship in the movie with the black d.j. was interesting. At one point, I thought you were going to take him into your confidence and get him to help you with your problem with the girl. The point when I realized this wouldn't happen was when you were sitting at the turntable talking to him while he was getting high in the dark, unseen—was that intentional?

EASTWOOD: No, though maybe I had underlying thoughts of it that way. I just thought that visually and emotionally it made more sense that the guy is contemplating out loud, he's got somebody to talk to. It was just so much better to take the other d.j. off than to cut back and forth. Dave, the character I play, just talks freely, thinks out loud. How do you do that when you're looking at somebody? The other guy is there and listening, but he won't help. Of course, he doesn't realize how serious the problem is, since Dave only takes him into his confidence to a certain degree. If he had taken him into his confidence more and been offered some profound advice, I would have brought the other guy into the scene more. Remember, Dave never tells the other guy any of the jazz about the suicide and homicide attempts.

KAMINSKY: The only comment the friend makes as he leaves is a joke, a sexual innuendo: "He who lives by the sword, dies by the sword." You do pretty nearly die by the sword [or a knife, technically] in *Misty*.

EASTWOOD: Well, I wrote that line. I did it years ago. There was this friend of mine who was hung up over a chick and trying to get her an abortion, and he was asking me for advice on the telephone. I told him what I thought he should do, and then he said: He who lives by the sword shall die by the sword. And I incorporated it into the films.

KAMINSKY: How did you come by that game business you did with Don Siegel in the bar scene?

EASTWOOD: It was made up by the writer, Dean Riesner. The moves were just improvised. I had brought in Dean Riesner, incidentally, to work with my role, which was a little soft in an earlier version. The character was apologizing to his girl for things, and he didn't pick up the other girl in the saloon. She picked him up. I just didn't think it was natural. I thought the problems with his girl friend needed some motivation, perhaps the fact that he gets hung up with a fan now and then—you know, d.j.'s in small towns are somewhat big fish in a small pond, and they do get a lot of activity. I thought it would be better if he thinks he's making a deal with the girl in the bar. Anyway, Riesner made up the game. It was certainly an interesting thing. The game does not exist in reality: it was just something Dave and the bartender made up to intrigue women to come over and watch.

KAMINSKY: How did you come to choose Jessica Walter as the psychopath?

EASTWOOD: Over the studio's dead body. No, I was looking at film on different gals, and I was looking at this film *The Group*, a movie made in 1965, which happened to have in it about three girls who were being pushed by their agents for *Misty*. One was Jessica Walter. She was very good in that film. She plays a frigid gal who talks about sex but is really turned off—and she's with this German guy who's trying to put the make on her and she starts this turn-off, and he just hauls off and slaps the shit out of her. And the look on her face, the transition she makes, the story on her face made me want to get her. I talked to the studio and they named a couple of people who were more well-known, people they could get deals on because business was slow, and I said: I don't want deals, I just want someone who is right for the part. Jessica has certain characteristics as an actress that just made me have a hunch that she would be right. I though she was very good in *Misty*.

KAMINSKY: What was Dave's motivation for going

in the door at the end after he sees the dead cop?

EASTWOOD: Well, I think the motivation is justified because the girlfriend is in there, and he thinks: Geez, if this is what happened to the cop, what has happened to this chick?

KAMINSKY: When the maid is slashed up by the psychotic girl, I expected her to die. Why did you have her live?

EASTWOOD: Well, if she [Jessica Walter] had killed someone, it would have been just too much that she was released. We'd have to make up some other reason for her getting on the loose again, and we just preferred release to, say, escape. Things like that do happen: there was a case in Palo Alto where a guy went up to a door and just stabbed the girl who answered. She lived, he was put away for treatment for about six months, then released, and the girl was not told. One day he accidentally ran into her at a supermarket, and she really freaked out.

KAMINSKY: It's interesting that the psychotic girl has no background.

EASTWOOD: I was advised by lots of people to put in background, but you know, we in the audience meet her the same time the protagonist meets her, and we see her unfold as he does. I didn't see any reason for a scene in which we find out that the mother treated her wrong, the father ran off, etc. When a person finds out that someone is screwed up, knifing maids and things, unless he's very interested in psychiatry, he's not interested in why she's screwed up; he just wants to get out. I think that audiences are smarter than a lot of producers think they are, and I think the audience will draw with you.

KAMINSKY: Did you want to feel that the protagonist was somehow being paid back for his selfish sexual behavior in the past by being stuck with her?

EASTWOOD: No, I don't think he's being chastised by divine scrutiny. It's just that he's been in some situations, and just when he tries to straighten his life, this comes as a sort of ironic thing. He probably could have handled the situation better if this other girl hadn't come back just at that time. The problems for him are complicated by the one showing up all the time when he wants to be with the other girl.

KAMINSKY: Did you purposely hold off on your physical confrontations with Jessica Walter? The only physically violent thing you do is hit her once, near the end, and of course it works, because the audience is so worked up against her too.

EASTWOOD: At the sneak preview, guys in the audience were saying: "Hit her, hit her." They were also with it throughout, saying things like: "Don't go in that door." That's very satisfying, but, yes, to answer the question, that's just the final thing. Here she is, she's killed a cop and is working him over—I mean, this is it.

*Play Misty for Me* was taken from a true story. The suicide attempt, the cutting up of the clothes, the attempt on Dave's life during the night all were taken from actual incidents (not the knifing of the maid, though, or the killing of the cop or the becoming roommates with the girl). The roommate part was stimulated by the fact that the woman in the real series of incidents would dress up, put on wigs, and go into saloons where the guy was drinking and keep an eye on him and see if he was trying to pick up someone.

KAMINSKY: Was this a story you knew or read or what?

EASTWOOD: Jo Heims, who wrote the story, worked it up, fictionalizing it. What appealed to me about the script is that there are incidents like this in everyone's life, to some degree, this whole thing of interpretation of commitment, or misinterpretation of commitment. A girl may say: Sure, I feel the same way; I don't want any part of marriage. But then next week, slowly, there's that kind of throwing a blanket over a person.

KAMINSKY: The constriction comes through very well.

EASTWOOD: It's a very important part of the film, because that's the thing that makes it personal to the audience as opposed to just a horror movie. If you've had any kind of experience in your life where somebody has just tried to move in too fast, or has just held on too hard; I think everybody has had something like that. It's something that could happen.

KAMINSKY: Yes, a psychological distortion of something we all feel.

EASTWOOD: A lot of times, with stories about psychotic people, there's no identification factor. In a picture like *Psycho,* the real highlights of the film are strictly the shock and the suspense. It was of course fabulous to have that scene where she sees the skeleton in the basement, but then they almost destroyed everything later with all that unnecessary exposition. Of course, that was eleven years ago, and they used more exposition then.

KAMINSKY: Obviously your picture will be compared to *Psycho,* and you yourself have just made one comparison. Were you thinking of comparisons when you made the film?

EASTWOOD: No, I certainly wasn't trying to duplicate *Psycho* in any way. I never saw it that way myself, other than the attacks. Those attacks could be sprung upon the audience with the same kind of suspense and energy as Hitchcock used, I thought, but other than that, I saw it as a story of constriction, the blanket thrown over one, the things we talked about before, the bound-in feeling, the frustration of trying to solve it and not being able to, of having to sit down and calm the person you want to escape from.

No exposition after that is necessary. I heard one person say that he thought the explanation about Tony Perkins by the psychiatrist at the end of *Psycho* was because they didn't want to make it seem like the lead had any homosexual motivation. Nowadays you wouldn't care.

KAMINSKY: The cutting in and out of the seascape and cliffs, which sort of work into the end—were they part of the original conception?

EASTWOOD: Well, L.A. has a hundred disc jockeys and stations. So, in the first place, I know that area where we shot. I live up there, and I knew a disc jockey up there. Disc jockeys know everybody in a small town. They're big stars in their areas. So here's a guy who is quite successful working for a small station in a small town, and he has ambitions to do television and better things, and this is all destroyed because of this relationship, too.

KAMINSKY: What about the seascapes, specifically? In editing, you keep coming back to sea, birds, and cliffs.

EASTWOOD: It's just because the sea is so much a part of the whole thing, not just because it was the place of the conclusion of her life [Jessica Walter].

KAMINSKY: The movie contains two breaks. First, when Jessica Walter goes to the hospital, there is that love sequence with the other girl, followed by the jazz-festival sequence. Both, I assume, are used to show passage of time, yet both go on longer than would be necessary just to show passage of time. Was it that you liked the sequences, or were you trying to make us forget about the mentally disturbed girl, or what?

EASTWOOD: A little of both. The real motive was temporarily to take us away from Evelyn [Jessica Walter]. People were also suggesting that the part of the other girl, Tobie, needed strengthening and there should be some sort of love scene. Well, I hated the idea of a dialogue sort of love scene, bullshit dialogue, and I was trying to look for a visual way to show life was really falling into place for these two people. I heard this song, "The First Time," going to work one day, on this FM station, and I said: God, that just tells the whole story, so I went out and bought the song, not just the song but the whole record and just took the master tape and played it, and I edited the scene to that, because I thought it told the whole story. There was nothing else around, no human life, aircraft, automobiles, etc. in that sequence. It showed that things were really working well for them. That was the only non-source music I used. Then we went to the jazz festival and back into his profession with a little bit of music, music which was more into the rhythm of the film, and then I figured: boom, I could go back to the station and the phone call. Bingo, here's this little fairy tale with a wrench stuck in the wheels.

KAMINSKY: There's one shot in there which is one of the most beautiful I've ever seen, and that is the orange-ish sea with the sun going down. But as far as plot in those two sequences, all we know is that Dave's girl has a new roommate.

EASTWOOD: Well, it's just a thing that grates on the guy. It was a very tough thing to set up that roommate thing without setting up so much that you tip it off. If you talk too much about it, you tip it off. So there has to be a first discussion of it, and then you meet one of them, and then there is the jazz festival, which is the last time roommates are mentioned. I had to do that in a very brief way. I don't doubt that a good percentage of the audience did guess what would happen.

KAMINSKY: I think the normal reaction is that when Tobie calls to the roommate and says, "Annabelle," what you expect is nobody to come out because Evelyn has killed Annabelle, but this isn't what happens. Evelyn walks out and is accepted as Annabelle.

EASTWOOD: Yes, that's when everybody starts lighting up their cigarettes.

KAMINSKY: I came into the movie cold, not knowing what it was about. Do you think that publicity and word of mouth will hurt the picture, and did you think of this in making the movie? The critics of course will screw things up too by giving away the plot and direction.

EASTWOOD: Yes, I have to hope that there's just enough entertainment value there regardless. If it is effective, even if they know what is going to happen, people will stay with it.

KAMINSKY: *Psycho* is an example of this: everybody knows what will happen, and it's exciting anyway.

EASTWOOD: Yes, the first thing everyone talks about is the shower sequence.

KAMINSKY: I was watching your knifing scenes closely, and you actually show a couple of slashes, unlike *Psycho,* though the feeling of revulsion and pain is similar.

EASTWOOD: Well, I just preferred to make it a little more ... maybe I'm not as subtle as Hitchcock is.

KAMINSKY: How long did it take you to make the film?

EASTWOOD: We shot it in four and a half weeks.

We have a five-week schedule. We were two and a half days under schedule.

KAMINSKY: Would you say it was expensive or inexpensive?

EASTWOOD: Inexpensive. We shot it completely away from the studio, one-hundred percent natural locations. We just rented houses, moved in, and shot. We rented a house for Dave, for example, and decorated it some, because there was stuff that had to be carved up and broken. Bob Daley is a very sharp guy on costs, and he didn't let too many false charges stack up. The studio would have liked it to have been even more expensive, but we were trying to prove something: that we could make something of entertainment value without exorbitant fees tacked on. I did have complete freedom on the picture, so if it doesn't work, it's my fault, and that's fine. I was given a chance to fail or do it right.

KAMINSKY: Do you do what Don tries: go for a usable take the first time?

EASTWOOD: Well, I do rehearse. I use a different technique than Don, a video-West technique. We used Panavision equipment, which goes through the same lens as the camera, and I can go back and look at the scene afterwards. Jerry Lewis uses a similar method, a TV camera which goes parallel with the movie camera. My method is superior in that even the focus is the same, so even if the focus operator misses the shot, you can see it. It's black and white, but you can see how the scene will be set up. It's terrific on zoom shots.

KAMINSKY: I also noticed that you use a lot of the people that Don Siegel uses, for example Carl Pingatore was your editor, Dean Riesner your writer, Bruce Surtees your cameraman.

EASTWOOD: Well, as far as Bruce goes, I'd worked with him three times as an operator, and Don and I promoted him for *The Beguiled,* which he did, but even before he did *The Beguiled,* Bruce was set for *Misty*: we had talked about it and he'd read the story.

KAMINSKY: You directed several sequences of *Dirty Harry*. Was that your first real experience of directing?

EASTWOOD: No, I had directed *Misty* first and also a short subject on Don Siegel. Actually, I can't take as much credit for directing the latter. The editor/writer was more or less the brains behind the thing. I thought it was pretty good. We slapped it together in about a day. Had to use still pictures and everything.

The reviews of *Play Misty for Me* were among the best Eastwood had received as an actor, and his debut as a director was generally admired, though there were strong dissenters.

Andrew Sarris in *The Village Voice* called the film "a surprisingly auspicious directorial debut for Clint Eastwood . . . one of the most effectively scary movies of this or any year."

Joseph Gelmis said in *Newsday*: "Eastwood's first crack at directing is remarkably effective. . . . Throughout, Eastwood resists overreaching [and] keeps his cool very nicely on both sides of the camera."

Most critics did complain about the idyllic sequence in which Eastwood and Miss Mills roamed about to the music of "The First Time Ever I Saw Your Face." Ironically, the song, which was several years old at the time, became a top hit of 1971 and 1972 after *Play Misty for Me* reintroduced it.

# CHAPTER EIGHT

# Dirty Harry Callahan

*Dirty Harry* was, only two years after its initial release, one of the most successful films of all time, beating out the total rentals on such financial bonanzas as *Planet of the Apes, Rosemary's Baby, True Grit, A Clockwork Orange,* and even such Walk Disney perennials as *Snow White* and *Pinocchio.* By January, 1974, *Dirty Harry* had brought Warner Brothers over sixteen million dollars in rentals to theaters in the United States alone.

Certainly, Eastwood's decision to make *Dirty Harry* was partly in reaction to the relatively poor reception of *The Beguiled.* He was searching for, and found, a straightforward, violent film.

The story and original script of *Dirty Harry* belonged to Warner Brothers. According to Jennings Lang, Universal Studios had at one time offered it to Paul Newman, who turned it down, saying that he couldn't play that kind of character. Originally, *Dirty Harry* was to be dirty, rumpled, cigar-chomping, and stubble-faced. Ironically, Newman suggested that Universal try to get Clint Eastwood for the role, and he, Newman would produce it. Universal couldn't decide who should produce it and eventually sold the script to Warner Brothers, who decided to use it as a vehicle for Frank Sinatra, with Irvin Kershner (*Up the Sandbox, Loving, The Flim-Flam Man*) directing. Sinatra was set to do the film, but was forced to change his mind because of a minor but incapacitating illness. At that point, Warner Brothers offered it to Clint Eastwood and Malpaso. Eastwood agreed, provided he could have Don Siegel as director.

Together Eastwood and Siegel, working with their favorite writer, Dean Riesner, changed the *Dirty Harry* script to fit Eastwood and Siegel's conception.

For example, in the original script, it was not Harry who confronted and shot the villain at the end of the film. The original script had the killer at an airport about to board the plane he demanded by holding hostages. An army sharpshooter is called upon to deliver the shot from a distance and save the hostages. The sharpshooter does so, and the film ends with a burning airplane and rumpled Harry in the good graces of the New York police department.

In the Siegel-Eastwood version, it is Harry who confronts the killer and defeats him. Perhaps because of Eastwood's bigger-than-life screen image, this is acceptable. We accept his taking everything into his own hands and are confident that he can do it. Another important change was in the location of the film. Siegel had shot an earlier film in San Francisco, *The Line-Up*, about a search by police for a mad killer. (That film, too, ended with a chase, confrontation, and shooting of the killer by the cop.) From Eastwood's perspective, San Francisco was home, the place where he had spent his high-school days, a location he knew well. In addition, Siegel and Eastwood had already done a cop-versus-mad-criminal film in New York, *Coogan's Bluff*. This was to be a more humorless tale, and they agreed on a totally different location. Finally, the film was based on an actual San Francisco incident.

There are, however, distinct similarities between Coogan and Harry. Both characters are described by their superiors as getting every dirty job in the book. Both Coogan and Harry lose their prisoners and feel responsible for getting them back. One important difference is that Coogan is doing it for his own pride, while Dirty Harry is doing it to a great degree because he feels responsible for the safety of San Francisco; he considers himself a one-man police force.

As Eastwood told *Playboy* magazine in an interview in the February, 1974, issue, his favorite role was probably Dirty Harry: "That's the kind of thing I like to think I can do as well as, or maybe better than, the next guy. He's very good at his job, and his individualism pays off to some degree. What I liked about playing that character was that he becomes obsessed; he's got to take his killer off the street."

In *Dirty Harry* as it was finally released, Andy Robinson plays a long-haired, mad killer somewhat similar to the Zodiac killer who terrorized San Francisco several years ago. The killer, who calls himself Scorpio, kills people from San Francisco rooftops with a high-powered rifle. He leaves notes for the police saying he will stop if he is given $200,000. The first detective to find the initial note is Dirty Harry Callahan, who sets out to catch the killer before he destroys more people. Callahan (Eastwood) and his new partner, Chico (Reni Santoni), try to trap the killer, but he evades them. In the course of searching for the killer, Eastwood stumbles into several other dirty jobs. At one point he foils a bank robbery which happens to take place while he is eating a hot dog across the street. At another point he volunteers to rescue a potential suicide from the ledge of a building. The pursuit of Scorpio, who eventually kills a policeman and a ten-year-old boy, continues. Scorpio then kidnaps a fourteen-year-old girl and demands immediate delivery of the ransom. The mayor, played by John Vernon, agrees to the demand, and Eastwood volunteers to make the delivery even though he and his superior Bressler, (Harry Guardino), are convinced the girl is dead. By a series of phone calls, Scorpio leads Eastwood around San Francisco and then meets him in a park, where he beats Eastwood savagely and informs him that the girl is dead. In the park battle, Chico is shot and seriously wounded by the killer as he attempts to help Eastwood. Eastwood manages to stab Scorpio in the leg with a knife he has taped to his leg.

After receiving minimal treatment—though his ribs are broken—Eastwood follows up a lead about a man with a knife wound. A doctor tells Eastwood that the man he wants is the groundskeeper at Keazar Stadium. The battered Eastwood climbs the stadium fence, breaks into Scorpio's room under the stands, pursues the killer onto the field, and after shooting him in the leg, tortures him to get him to tell where the girl is. The girl's body is found but Scorpio is released because his rights have been violated by Eastwood and the evidence obtained is all inadmissible.

Convinced that Scorpio will kill again, Eastwood follows him constantly. To get rid of his pursuer, the mad killer pays to have himself savagely beaten so he can blame the policeman. Eastwood is ordered to stop following Scorpio. Immediately, Scorpio captures and terrorizes a school bus and the young children on it. He stops briefly, calls the mayor, and demands money and a plane out of the country. The mayor agrees, but Eastwood, knowing Scorpio well by now, is sure that he will kill the children. Though he is told to stay out of the case, Eastwood heads off the bus, jumps on top of it from a bridge, and after a brief chase, shoots and kills Scorpio, who is holding a young boy at gunpoint. Knowing that he has again disobeyed orders, Eastwood throws away his badge, and the picture ends.

*Dirty Harry* is an exploration of man and his uncontrolled self. The killer in *Dirty Harry* is totally mad. He is nameless, intent on the wanton destruction of society. His violence is hideous. He opens the film with the murder of an innocent woman (perhaps retribution for the female devourers of Siegel and Eastwood's *Two Mules* and *The Beguiled*). He then kills a small boy, a young girl. He goes after a priest and finally settles on a busload of children. It is all society that he wishes to destroy without compromise. The Eastwood character, in contrast, is a bigot, a willful killer who likes his dirty work and is out to avenge the death of his wife. He appears to have no home, to exist only so that he can destroy with his oversize Magnum pistol, a protagonist again retreating into nonemotion, as earlier Eastwood film heroes. The two extremes must settle the world between them, and all of society—the judge, the public—must stand aside and watch fate resolved in the clash of two madnesses. Our sympathy is clearly with Eastwood, however, who in destroying Scorpio is also performing an act for the benefit of society, while Scorpio's acts are totally monstrous. By the time of their final confrontation, Eastwood has given hints that he might be willing to try again, willing to feel, but the hints are small, almost indiscernible and almost exclusively attached to a feeling for his wounded partner and his wife. When Eastwood and Scorpio meet, they are beyond society, beyond law. Eastwood has been told not to confront the killer, to give in to all his demands. To Eastwood, that is chaos and an unsatisfactory conclusion. He must face the killer. After he destroys Scorpio, Eastwood throws his badge away. He has gone beyond the confines of law and society, and will surely be fired or will quit. There is no happy ending for him, no feeling, no function. When the camera zooms slowly back to leave him, he is alone and lost. We can conceive of no future for him, though there was to be in *Magnum Force*.

Director Don Siegel calls the film a "wall-to-wall carpet of violence." "In *Dirty Harry*," says Siegel, "Clint was a hard-nosed cop who believed that what he was doing was right. It doesn't mean that Clint and I agree with the character one hundred percent. Harry is a racist, a reactionary. Yet policemen do lose their lives protecting us, and it has nothing to do with politics. Some policemen are like Harry, genuine heroes whose attitudes I abhor. Maybe there would be no problem or need for them if there were no violence in the world, but there is."

In fact, positive police reaction to *Dirty Harry* has continued to roll in to both Eastwood and Siegel. On one hand, a police department in the Philippines asked for a 16-mm print of the film to use in training its force. In addition, both Siegel and Eastwood have been asked to speak before police groups and organizations. Both men have turned down such invitations in the belief that they are filmmakers, not political forces.

But Pauline Kael, the *New Yorker*'s film critic and author of *I Lost It at the Movies,* has called *Dirty Harry* fascist. Other critics have agreed, though the critic for *Rolling Stone,* a superliberal magazine, loved the film, and *Time*'s film critic, Jay Cocks, named it one of the ten best films of 1971.

Both Siegel and Eastwood are bothered by the accusations about the film's political conservativism.

"I don't think *Dirty Harry* was a fascist picture," says Eastwood. "It's just the story of one frustrated police officer in a frustrating situation on one particular case. It showed the frustrations of the job, but it wasn't a glorification of the police."

Eastwood's argument about the basis of *Dirty Harry* being not about a political position but about one man's obsession has ample support in the history of fiction and film. The traditional police-procedure film has dealt with the detective's increasing obsession with capturing a particular criminal. It goes far beyond any political struggle and into a classical confrontation between two men destined to meet in a deadly showdown. Certainly no one talks about *Les Miserables* and detective Javert's obsessive pursuit of Jean Valjean as being fascist. But it is essentially the same idea as that which exists in *Dirty Harry, Coogan's Bluff, The French Connection, Bullitt,* and dozens of other stories.

The essence of *Dirty Harry,* however, is action and violence. Scenes and lines in the film are hard to erase from one's memory. For example, the thwarting of the bank robbery—the only sequence shot at Universal Studio and not on location in San Francisco—involved split-second timing and the destruction of a fire hydrant with Eastwood approaching the wounded robber while he continues to chew his hot dog. Advancing on the robber, who is tempted to reach for his gun and shoot the approaching cop, Eastwood softly mutters: "The thing is, you're not really sure whether I fired five or six. And if five, whether or not I keep one under the hammer." Eastwood smiles slightly and then continues enjoying the conversation. "Tell you the truth, I lost count myself. Now, what you got to do, considering this is a forty-four Magnum, the most powerful hand gun in the world and will blow your head off if it's loaded . . ." The robber looks uncertain and seems tempted to reach for his gun, and Eastwood continues, "What you've got to do is ask yourself, 'Are you feeling lucky, punk?' " The robber gives up, and then, torn with curiosity, asks Eastwood to let him know if there is another bullet in the gun. With a smile, Eastwood points the gun at the man, who pulls in his breath. He fires, but the gun is empty.

The scene is definitive Eastwood. In the midst of violence on a busy street, he confidently plays out a game, a traditional Western movie game of how-many-bullets-did-he-fire? We are sure that Harry knows all the time that there are no bullets left, but he is supremely confident. It is his violent world, a world in which he talks softly and carries a big gun.

Later, when he faces Scorpio in a similar situation and says the same words, there is no humor behind them. He knows this time that there is a bullet left, but this time he is not just playing a violent game. It is the last game.

Although he was in the process of working on *Play Misty for Me* while *Dirty Harry* was being shot, Eastwood's experience as a director had been minimal. At one point in the shooting of *Harry*, Siegel developed a cold and was laid up for a few days. Eastwood directed two sequences in the film, a confrontation with a homosexual in the park and the rescue of the would-be suicide. The latter was a particularly complex situation involving the hoisting of Eastwood on a fireman's rig and night-time shooting.

Director Siegel liked the scene, and none but the most critical film scholars can detect a difference. Indeed, the two men worked so closely together on the film that it is hard to tell where one's contribution began and the other's took over.

One of Eastwood's most direct contributions was in the performing of stunts. One stunt in particular caused Siegel anxiety. It involved Harry Callahan jumping from a bridge trestle to the top of the school bus being driven by Scorpio. Siegel wanted to use a double. Eastwood wanted to do the stunt himself.

"Not," pointed out Eastwood, "that I like to do dangerous things, though I did do quite a few in earlier films, but that if I didn't do that stunt and the viewers didn't see during the jump that it was actually me, they wouldn't believe it. The thrill and identification are greater when they know it is the star doing the stunt."

That is one reason why, in a Clint Eastwood film, when he is riding on top of the hood of a speeding car, as in *Magnum Force,* or *Thunderbolt and Lightfoot,* leaping from a bridge, as in *Dirty Harry,* or speeding through a park on a motorcycle, as in *Coogan's Bluff,* there will always be at least one or two shots making it quite clear that Eastwood has done at least a significant part of that stunt.

*Dirty Harry* had other problems, some of them stemming from location shooting in San Francisco and shooting at night. After all, people are not likely to be tolerant of machine guns being fired over their heads.

"It was very tricky and very physical," recalls Eastwood.

"And an added problem was the fact that we

110

couldn't work past midnight because of the gun-fire," added Siegel.

Siegel and Eastwood are somewhat puzzled by the reaction to a tall neon rooftop "Jesus Saves" sign they had made, which is destroyed during a gun battle between Dirty Harry and Scorpio. The forty-foot, multicolored sign was arranged for by the film's art director, Dale Hennessey.

"People have complained about that neon sign in the film, though it's hard to know why it offends them," muses Siegel. According to Siegel and Eastwood, the sign has no particular significance, at least no conscious significance. "We needed something to draw interest to that roof when we shifted attention to the killer," said Siegel.

When it is pointed out to Eastwood that, unlike *The Beguiled,* which was filled with females, *Dirty Harry* has almost none, and no sexual interest, Eastwood replies, "No female lead at all. It's kind of a Western. There's no time for a love interest, which would only interrupt the suspense. Besides, Don and I had all we wanted of women in *The Beguiled,* where I had my hands full playing opposite eight females."

During the shooting of *Dirty Harry,* Eastwood was approached by more fans than usual, partly because he was shooting on location in a big city rather than in the wilds of Mexico or Spain or in a small town.

Although he occasionally tires of the pressure of fans, Eastwood is rather good-natured about it and recognizes that he is dependent on these fans for his success. A primary problem, however, of being

111

recognized, according to Eastwood, is that it becomes difficult for him to observe people and incorporate what he observes into his creativity as an actor or director.

"They watch me instead of me watching them," he says. To go out with any degree of anonymity, Eastwood has occasionally put on dark glasses and a false moustache. Most of the time, however, he remains near his home in Carmel, where people have gradually grown accustomed to seeing him on the streets.

He has allowed his privacy to be invaded for the sake of promotion of his films or to accommodate sincere fans. For example, he allowed a Japanese film crew recently to follow him around for weeks to make a documentary on his work for the fans who have been loyal to him since the *Rawhide* year.

A glimpse of Eastwood in public was provided in the July 23, 1971, cover story of *Life,* in which the writer, who watched a day of shooting, observed: "As always when he appears in public, fans come up in twos and threes, paper and pencils extended. He stops for every one, good-naturedly asking names and chatting briefly. One young Japanese boy comes up to him shyly with a copy of *Mad* magazine, and Clint breaks into a grin as he sees himself in comic-book caricatures entitled 'Fistful of Lasagne' and 'For a Few Ravioli More.' "

The *Life* writer observed that, "Like the character he plays, Eastwood feels most comfortable in the all-male world of beers, admiring women, and uncomplicated language."

Eastwood also told *Life* that he feels a lot of actors have gotten too involved in trying to make message pictures instead of entertainments like *Dirty Harry*.

"There's nobody in the theater to get the message," said Eastwood. "You have to have good entertainment first. If I started to pay too much attention to what the reviewers say, I'd have an ulcer."

The film, indeed, was released first and foremost as an entertainment, as exemplified by the following bits and pieces of press information on *Dirty Harry* from Warner Brothers:

"Don Siegel, who directed Clint Eastwood's *Dirty Harry* for Warner Brothers, shot several scenes at the Roaring Twenties, a nudie bar on San Francisco's Broadway. Right next door was another palace of nudity, Big Al's, in front of which stood a barker hustling midday customers. 'Come in,' he urged, 'and see what the movie leaves out.'"

"Inspector Ken Manley of the Homicide Bureau, San Francisco Police Department, missed two days of his assignment as technical adviser for *Dirty Harry* . . . while he testified in a murder case. He returned to the Clint Eastwood starrer to discover he had missed three set murders."

"Lolita Rios, Janet Wisely, and Laury Monk played naked ladies in *Dirty Harry*. . . . The girls are more or less typecast, since they work as naked ladies six nights a week at a nudie joint in the location town of San Francisco."

"The blood in a swimming pool in a scene for *Dirty Harry* isn't blood at all. It's a red concoction with an oil base put together by Warner's special-effects men. On camera it looks like the real thing, but in real life it can be scooped out of the pool like seaweed, leaving the pool free of contamination and saving cleaning and draining."

Most of the critics ignored such fascinating bits of information and concentrated on disliking the film, while millions ignored them and saw it. Jay Cocks in *Time* was an exception: "Eastwood gives his best performance so far—tense, tough, full of implicit identification with his character. . . . The kind of movie that brightens up Hollywood's tarnished name."

Paul D. Zimmerman in *Newsweek* was less enthusiastic about the film, acknowledging, however, that "what seems like a political statement is at heart just a plot device." Zimmerman concluded, "*Dirty Harry* has upset some political liberals and moderates, but there is little chance that this rightwing fantasy will change things where decades of humanists films have failed."

The final word, however, goes to Paul Nelson, writing about Eastwood and *Dirty Harry* in *Rolling Stone*. In the March 2, 1972, issue, Nelson attacked Pauline Kael, Vincent Canby, and others who had labeled *Dirty Harry* a fascist film, an immoral film.

"In radical 1972," wrote Nelson, "the idea of a cop-as-genre-hero seems subversive to many, and, as a result, both Siegel's primary intentions and the nature of Eastwood's character have been widely misunderstood and badly distorted. . . . By the movie's end, Harry Callahan seems an archetype of the action hero adrift at the end of the 1960's, a man first and a political symbol not at all, as dignified, as honorable, and yet as out of place in today's world as are William Holden, Ernest Borgnine, Warren Oates, and Ben Johnson in theirs at the close of Sam Peckinpah's *The Wild Bunch.*

"All of the movie's action," Nelson continued, "of course, revolves around the character of Dirty Harry himself, and Clint Eastwood's remarkably subtle, fluid portrayal expertly delineates the ironic duality of the man. . . . The film's quietest moments . . . can be convincingly welded to its most corrosive . . . chiefly because of the controlled brilliance of the performance of Eastwood, who promises to be a major force in the films of the next decade, both as an actor and a director."

# CHAPTER NINE

# Back to the Ponchos

*Joe Kidd* returned Clint Eastwood to the West and the unshaven image of his earlier films. The film was directed by one of the most respected directors of Westerns in Hollywood, John Sturges, whose credits include *Bad Day at Black Rock, Gunfight at the O.K. Corral, The Magnificent Seven, The Great Escape,* and *Marooned.* Sturges had directed such stars as Spencer Tracey, Lee Marvin, Burt Lancaster, Steve McQueen, Charles Bronson, James Coburn, Gene Hackman, Gregory Peck, and Richard Widmark. His films frequently have dealt with men isolated against great odds. In *Black Rock,* Tracy has to overcome a gang including Robert Ryan, Ernest Borgnine, and Lee Marvin, even though he has only one arm. In *Gunfight at the O.K. Corral,* the Earps must defeat the Clanton gang. In *The Magnificent Seven,* the Seven, led by Yul Brunner and McQueen, must defeat a huge gang of Mexican bandits. In *The Great Escape,* James Garner and McQueen must escape from a tightly guarded Nazi prison camp. And in *Marooned,* the isolation and odds are even greater. Three astronauts—Gene Hackman, Richard Crenna, and James Franciscus—are

116

trapped in a spaceship orbiting earth. They are gradually running out of air while rescue efforts go on and they learn to rely on themselves.

*Joe Kidd* is similar to the other Sturges-directed films of strong individuals isolated against tremendous odds. In this case, Eastwood takes on the role of whole gangs in the earlier Sturges films. He needs no help.

At the beginning of the film, Joe Kidd (Eastwood) is a grubby, dirty semi-barfly in the small town of Sinola, New Mexico, where a trial of some outlaws is taking place. Eastwood is also on trial for a minor offense. A gang of Mexican bandits led by Luis Chama (John Saxon) rescues the outlaws. Eastwood, who is known as a great tracker, is recruited to hunt them down after he discovers that the Mexicans have stolen his horses and killed one of his men. (How the grubby creature acquired horses and men is never made quite clear.) Actually, his recruitment comes after a band of mercenaries with high-powered rifles joins the hunt with murderous intent. Under the direction of a vengeance-minded landowner (Robert Duvall), Eastwood, now clean-shaven, and two others (Don Stroud and James Wainright) set out to find Chama. The landowner quickly establishes the extent of his villainy when he warns Mexicans he encounters that "We can cut your ears off, and we can cut something else off too."

Eastwood begins to sympathize with the Mexicans and Chama, who have claimed that all their actions were a result of being cheated by the landowner, whose brutality against the Mexican helps settle the issue for Kidd.

The turning point comes when the landowner takes over a small Mexican town and threatens to kill everyone in it if Chama does not give up. When Eastwood realizes that Chama has no intention of giving up, he decides to rescue the town and do battle with the landowner and his men.

Eastwood does defeat the villains and brings Chama into town, where the law is waiting under the landowner's orders to gun them down. The climax of the film comes when a huge locomotive carrying Eastwood comes crashing through the wall of the bar in which we had seen him at the start of the film. The destruction is tremendous and the sudden appearance of the huge machine through the wall is spectacular.

In some ways, *Joe Kidd* is reminiscent of the Leone Westerns. As in *A Fistful of Dollars,* for example, the Eastwood character finds himself between two rivals and their gangs. Ultimately, neither side is worth joining. They are both corrupt and evil for different reasons. Eastwood, as superhero, has to step in and overcome both sides. However, in the Sturges film, unlike the Leone film, Eastwood does it all without trickery. He is direct and openly committed to humanity.

Jay Cocks in *Time* dismissed the film as a "leisurely Eastwood Western in which the star is presumably recuperating from the rigors of his recent *Dirty Harry* and *Play Misty for Me.*" As for the locomotive crashing through the wall, Cocks thought, "The set seems to have been constructed solely with this event in mind, looking as it does like something plucked from the window of F.A.O. Schwarz."

Arthur Knight, in *Saturday Review,* saw "frightening implications" in the script of *Joe Kidd.* "Its creators," wrote Knight, "are men who have no sympathies, no commitments; for them, the entire world is corrupt. And the man they have chosen as their hero, Joe Kidd, in his single-minded purpose of turning the corrupt Mexican over to a corrupt justice, is demonstrably mad."

It might be argued that Knight, indeed, has not just outlined Eastwood's character in Joe Kidd, but Eastwood's character in almost all of his action films, a man who sees the world as corrupt, a man who is single-mindedly determined to defeat that corruption by himself. To do so takes a superman, a man with determined madness and dedication, an avenging angel.

*Joe Kidd* is a box-office success. By the beginning of 1974, the film had earned over six million dollars in the United States alone, placing it in earnings ahead of *Play Misty for Me* ($5,375,000), *Kelly's Heroes* ($5,135,000), and *Two Mules for Sister Sara* ($4,900,000).

Eastwood's next film, *High Plains Drifter,* was his second effort at directing and his first direction of a Western.

Eastwood-directed films are identifiable so far by their weather-report titles: *Play Misty for Me, Drifter,* and *Breezy. Drifter* is perhaps the stormiest of the group.

In numerous interviews since his *Rawhide* days, Eastwood has referred to himself as a drifter, a drifter not unlike the man in his film. That the film also seems to refer to both the Leone films he did and the Siegel Westerns is not coincidental. A striking reminder of Eastwood's awareness of his references can be seen in a publicity still for the movie. In the still, Eastwood and Verna Bloom are standing over a grave in the cemetery that plays an important part in the film. Eastwood is leaning on the gravestone with his left hand and holding his hat over his heart with his right. The name on the stone is "Donald Siegel." Slightly behind this grave is another, the stone on which reads "S. Leone."

It is a good example of Eastwood's quiet humor. Both stones appear in the film, but neither is visible long enough to read. The reference is personal for Eastwood, a joke, and, at the same time, a burying of the two personalities with which he has been most identified.

*High Plain Drifter* is like a Leone-Siegel film which Eastwood makes his own.

The similarities start with the opening of the strange film. The Stranger (the Eastwood character has no name), unshaven, wearing a long coat, rides into a small town near a beautiful lake. Apparently he is after only a shave and a bath, but he winds up killing three men who decide to pick on the quiet stranger.

It seems the three men had been hired by the town to protect it from another trio of gunmen who were about to be released from prison and who, the townspeople are sure, will come and destroy the town that arranged to send them up on a charge of stealing from the mining company that runs the town.

The town immediately begins to implore the Eastwood character to save them from the ex-cons.

After many strange demands, including one that the townspeople will do anything he wishes, Eastwood accepts the job.

With the aid of the town dwarf (Billy Curtis), Eastwood begins to prepare the defenses of the town, but each defense and demand reveals the hypocrisy of the community. Once again, as in the Leone films and the Sturges film, he finds himself between two corrupt forces, the bandits and the townspeople. Eastwood's humiliation of the town is total. He rapes, ridicules, and impoverishes the townspeople, who, at one point, attempt, unsuccessfully, to get rid of him. Finally, he orders them to paint the entire town red and set up a huge feast, which they do as he rides out, apparently with no intention of engaging the trio of excons, led by Stacey Bridges (Geoffrey Lewis). The climax of the film comes in the town itself, which Eastwood has renamed "Hell." While the town is burning, Bridges and his helpers track down and destroy the mining-company bosses.

Just as it seems that they will destroy everyone, Eastwood reappears and destroys the trio while Hell burns in a sequence remarkably like one in an old William S. Hart film, *Hell's Hinges*. He also makes it clear that he is not a human being at all but an avenging ghost, the ghost of the sheriff of the town, who had been killed before the film began by the trio and who had received no help from the town.

The film ends with Eastwood as the ghostly rider being lost in the mist of the plains.

The burning scene is similar to that in *A Fistful of Dollars*, as is the entire handling of the broad outdoor scenes and the operatic hero who is bigger than life. In this case, the Eastwood character is so much bigger than life that he is, indeed, a ghost, or an avenging angel.

Eastwood believes *High Plains Drifter* is similar to *High Noon*, the film in which the actor with whom he is frequently compared, Gary Cooper, has to battle a trio of returning convicts (one of whom, coincidentally, was played by Lee Van Cleef) who are bent on killing him.

"That community didn't want to get involved, either," noted Eastwood in his *Playboy* interview with Arthur Knight. "They weren't totally evil, they were just complacent, and they just sat back and let their marshal get whipped to death." Eastwood sees both films as comments on a problem of contemporary society, the fear of getting involved.

In an article he wrote for *Action,* the magazine of the Directors Guild of America, Eastwood said of *High Plains Drifter* that it had the longest schedule of any film he had so far directed.

The film was shot on Mono Lake in the Sierras, a location picked by Eastwood, and an entire town had to be constructed there. Since the town had to be destroyed by fire at the end of the film, the film had to be shot in continuity. Normally a film is shot with all the scenes in one location done at the same time. Later, the various scenes are put together by an editor according to a script and under the supervision of the director. By shooting the scenes in one location first, it is often possible to let some actors finish all of their work on a film very quickly. Since this couldn't be done for *High Plains Drifter*—the town could be destroyed only once, and all scenes before its destruction had to be shot before it was destroyed—the actors had to stay on salary for a long time.

The big advantage of shooting the film in continuity, according to Eastwood, was that it speeded up the editing of the film, which often takes months.

With all the complications of shooting, Eastwood managed to finish the film's shooting in six weeks, two days less than he had allocated for the project.

"I must confess," he wrote, "that I can't stand long locations or production schedules. Once you get moving, I don't see any reason to drag your feet. During production, I can function much more fully and efficiently if I move full blast. Maybe it's because I'm basically lazy. For me, there is no happy medium."

Reviewers and critics were quick to see the relationship between the Eastwood character in *High Plains Drifter* and his nameless stranger in the Leone films.

Kevin Thomas in the *Los Angeles Times* called it "a stylized, allegorical Western of much chillingly paranoid atmosphere and considerable sardonic humor that confirms Eastwood's directorial flair. It is also a pretty violent business that won't disappoint the millions who flocked to the Leone Westerns."

In the first year of its release, *High Plains Drifter* earned $7,125,000 in the United States alone, putting it ahead of such films in the big-time figures as *Z, Shaft, Frenzy,* and *Dr. No.*

*High Plains Drifter* may be a one-shot example

in Eastwood's career. The other films he has directed have been low-budget works, modest, and unselfconscious. *Drifter* was a big-budget film with a large cast and a very self-conscious style. It was as if Eastwood had to get this film out to show that he could be in total control of the kind of film for which he had become famous. Both the critical response to the film and the box-office reception proved that he could.

Thus proved, Eastwood turned to his next project, a film which he would direct but in which he would not star.

# CHAPTER TEN

# A September Affair, and Dirty Harry Rides Again

*Breezy* is the first film with which Eastwood has been associated in which he does not appear. *Breezy*, starring William Holden and Kay Lenz, was produced and directed by Eastwood. It is also the only Eastwood film to date which has not made money. In fact, the 1973 film has had a cool critical and a cold public response.

In the film, Frank Harmon (William Holden) is a fifty-year-old California real-estate man who is bitter and disillusioned following his divorce from a bitchy woman, Paula (Joan Hotchkis). He wants to be left alone to wander around his Laurel Canyon semi-mansion. He meets a seventeen-year-old hippie-orphan, Breezy (Kay Lenz), who informs him that she is from Intercourse, Pennsylvania, that she loves him, and that she expects nothing from him. She takes refuge with Harmon because she is fleeing from a dirty old man (Norman Bartold) who is pursuing her.

At first Harmon spurns the girl, but when his ex-girl friend (Marj Dusay) loses her new husband in an auto crash, he decides that a short time with the girl is better than no time at all, and the problem of the age difference is left up in the air as the film ends.

In several ways, the film is a reversal of Eastwood's first-directed film, in which a woman determinedly pursues the protagonist. The screenplay is even by the same writer, Jo Heims. The reversal is that instead of being destructive in her pursuit of the man, the girl in *Breezy* is constructive, urging him to accept life instead of seeking to destroy it.

According to Holden, he thoroughly enjoyed working with Eastwood and would do it again. "I'd forgotten," says Holden, "what it is like to make pictures this agreeable. I'll work with Clint anytime he asks. Besides, he can't pull any crap on me, because he's an actor too.

"He's also even-tempered, a personality trait not much in evidence among directors. The crew is totally behind him, and that really helps things go smoothly. There has been no temperament, no nothing. We all do our work, and that's it."

As for directing a film in which he doesn't appear, Eastwood says, "It's definitely a lot easier. I didn't mind doing both on *High Plains Drifter*, because it's a Western, and I know Westerns pretty well. This film, however, was a love story. I'd never done a love story, so I stayed behind the camera."

*Breezy* was shot entirely in and around Los Angeles. Like other Eastwood films, it finished three days ahead of schedule, also a characteristic feat of director Don Siegel.

In making the film, Eastwood employed the

principles that he had adopted in his earlier works as director.

"One of the first lessons I learned—and I learned it quickly—during the shooting of *Misty*," wrote Eastwood in his *Action* article, "was that by keeping everybody involved in what you, the director, are doing, crews will work twice as hard and develop a tremendous esprit de corps. If you explain what effect you're striving for, instead of saying merely, 'Put that case over there,' or 'Set up that lamp down there,' your crew will become totally involved.

"My second lesson," wrote Eastwood, "was to be carefully prepared and well organized, but yet remain flexible, so that we could move from set to set easily and without strain."

*Variety* responded to the film by saying that the script has "too much laugh, smile, and chuckle sitcom patter and situation makes the film more like a television feature (where people too often have 'happy problems') than a tripping and certainly relevant (as always) sudser. Eastwood's roles have usually found him as a taciturn avenger or victim; in this type of story he must, as director, encourage his players to express far more emotions. There are a few flashes, so he's on his way. Maybe next time."

*Variety* also pointed out that the film is R-rated. "The domestic R rating," stated *Variety*, "would appear to derive from much breast nudity, not really needed and perhaps a b.o. [box office] hindrance in certain locations."

Eastwood's response was that *Breezy* did not deserve an R rating. "But," he says, "it is because some twenty states have statutes that say showing the nipple on a woman's breast to children is obscene. Why should that be considered obscene?"

The review in *Hollywood Reporter* generally reflected the response of the press in the comment that: "To Eastwood's credit, the acting and casting throughout are fine, particularly in light of Heim's overarch dialogue and easy philosophizing. But one never really believes that Holden and Lenz are in love; there's little passion, only slick and obvious manipulation with romps at the ocean and the like."

Whatever the reason, *Breezy* bombed, and Clint Eastwood immediately turned to a sure-fire success to hold onto his audience and his action reputation. The sure-fire success was *Magnum Force,* the sequel to *Dirty Harry.* This time out, however, the director was Ted Post, not Donald Siegel, who was committed to another project at the time.

*Magnum Force* starts with a reference to *Dirty Harry.* The credits appear next to a hand, Eastwood's, holding the huge Magnum pistol that was his trademark in the earlier film. As the credits end, the gun is pointed toward the camera, and Eastwood's voice repeats his Dirty Harry lines: "This is a 44 Magnum. The world's most powerful hand gun, and it will blow your head into little pieces. What you've got to do is ask yourself, are you feeling lucky?" With that, the gun fires and starts what is certainly the most violent of Eastwood's films. As in *Dirty Harry,* the movie opens with a murder. This time, instead of an innocent girl, the victim is a gangster/labor leader who has just been acquitted of murdering a rival and his family. The gangster and a car full of his fellow mobsters are murdered by a traffic policeman with a Magnum. At the scene of the murder, Eastwood informs his superior (with whom he does not get along ) that he would like to be on the case, that he *should* be on the case. The superior, Lieutenant Briggs, played by Hal Holbrook, refuses.

Eastwood and his partner, this time a young black man, then go to the airport, where a hijacking happens to be taking place. The idea is very much like the intrusion of the bank robbery in *Dirty Harry*. Harry (Eastwood) takes the pilot's place and in a shoot-out kills the hijackers.

Harry then encounters a fellow policeman, who seems a bit unhinged about the criminals who get away with murder. Harry begins to suspect that the man, McCoy, may be the murderer, especially when a series of murders of other gangsters and criminals follows the initial killing. At the same time, Harry meets a quartet of young, sharpshooting traffic policemen who clearly admire him and his reputation for shooting first and asking questions later.

The reputation is confirmed when Harry and his partner thwart a robbery and destroy the robbers. Meanwhile, Harry has time for a quick trip to bed with a Chinese girl who lives in his apartment building. Like the wife of McCoy a few scenes earlier, the girl asks Harry to go to bed with her. Sex, though not particularly emotional or part of the story, does appear, as it had not in *Dirty Harry*.

After further murders, and the killing of

McCoy, the cop he had suspected, Harry gradually comes to the realization that the killers are the four young traffic policemen. He sets up a trap to get a bullet from the Magnum of the best shooter of the group so that he can check it against the bullets that had killed the various criminals.

Eventually, the killer policemen realize that Harry is closing in on them after a trap that he sets up results in the death of one of the quartet. They ask Harry to join them in their campaign to rid the city of criminals. Harry says no, that he does not believe in cops going outside the law even if he has trouble accepting the Establishment and its ideas.

An attempt is then made to blow Harry up with a bomb, and while his partner is falling victim to a bomb, Harry calls Lieutenant Briggs to tell him that he has the confessions of the policemen and they are trying to kill him. Briggs arrives and reveals that he is the leader of the police group that plans to kill the criminals. In a car with Briggs, Harry disarms the lieutenant, dumps him out, and a chase begins between the three killer cops on motorcycles and Harry in his car. The chase ends in a huge abandoned ship, with Harry destroying the trio and disposing of Briggs, who reappears, with the bomb originally intended for Harry.

Although Eastwood is again playing Harry, he seems a much more open, emotional person than he had in the Siegel-directed film. He deals with women, has time for jokes, even indicates that he has friends.

Essentially, the film appears at first glance as a

kind of answer to the above-the-law attitude of Harry in the earlier film. In fact, he is just as much outside the law in *Magnum Force* as he had been in *Dirty Harry*. This time, however, the film appears to be more liberal because the object of Harry's lawlessness is a conspiracy of cops, a fascist group within the police department.

According to director Post, "*Magnum Force* is the closest I've come to getting an entertaining story that really has something important to say about where society is at.

"In *Dirty Harry*, Clint played a cop who felt that the law and courts were violating the safety of the citizens and making the job of a policeman next to impossible. Pauline Kael called it a fascist masterpiece, and that annoyed Clint.

"In *Magnum Force*, he's still Dirty Harry Callahan, but this time he takes a stand on the side of democracy versus a fascist Nazi-like element in the police force who decide to take the law into their own hands. It's a provocative, intelligent, controversial picture and anyone who just sees exploitative violence and sensationalism is very shallow."

Although Eastwood and Post knew each other well and worked well together on the film, Eastwood's experience as a director often made itself known. For example, at one point in the film Post patiently tried to get an inexperienced actress playing a stewardess to do what he wanted with an action, a minor action. Eastwood became impatient after a few minutes and interrupted to say to Post, "You're overintellectualizing things."

As with all films, problems arose. Cable cars that were supposed to appear in one scene did not show up and held up production. Actors clashed. Eastwood got stuck in a car and had to crawl out through a window to complete a scene, but the problems were minor.

The film was released, and in the first week of its showing in 401 theaters it grossed almost seven million dollars, a staggering record which it continued. Warner Brothers and Eastwood looked forward to the future and a double-bill release of both Dirty Harry films and even bigger box office records.

At the peak of his popularity, Clint Eastwood has also recently released another action film in which he stars, *Thunderbolt and Lightfoot,* and has plunged into the role, perhaps the biggest of his career, as the cool, urbane protagonist of the film version of the best-selling novel, *The Eiger Sanction.*

Privately, he remains somewhat of a puzzle. At home Eastwood wears six-dollar jeans and T shirts and drives a Chevrolet pickup truck, even though he owns a Ferarri and Norton and a number of Triumph motorcycles. Surprisingly, Eastwood has noted that unlike many stars, he is seldom pestered by fans when he appears in public.

Arthur Knight has said that "though Eastwood is the world's hottest star, it's hard to believe he believes it. And it's difficult to reconcile the real Clint Eastwood—gentle, soft-spoken, self-effacing—with the violent men he's played on screen, men who were ready to shoot first and talk later, if at all."

Although attempts have been made by various columnists to find a playboy image for Eastwood, he has evaded this easy peg also and remained a basically contented married man who recently celebrated his twentieth wedding anniversary. Of his wife, he said, "I'd say I'd have to give Mag a lot of credit. She's a bright girl, and she's interested in a lot of things I'm interested in. We were physically attracted, but we also had everything in common. We both liked the same kind of music—jazz and classical, like Bach. Most important, we are friends."

Others have attempted to pin a political label on Eastwood, but he responds, "I'm a political nothing. I mean, I hate to be categorized. I'm certainly not an extremist; the best thing you can say about extremists, either right or left, is that they're boring people."

Even his eating habits run to the unspectacular. He never eats cake, ice cream, or frozen vegetables. He prefers organically grown vegetables and breakfasts on grapefruit juice and white raisins. A typical Eastwood lunch is usually a tuna fish sandwich, a slice of avocado, some alfalfa sprouts, and an oatmeal cookie.

The boy who used to be farmed out to live with his grandmother in a wooden house on a mountain near Livermore, California, when his father couldn't support the family, is at the top of his profession and one of the world's truly rich men.

He is now a member, by appointment by the President, to the National Council on the Arts, representing the motion picture industry. He and his wife also sponsor the annual Clint Eastwood Invitational Tennis Tournament at Pebble Beach Country Club, with proceeds going to their favorite charities: the United Fund, the Behavioral Sciences Institute, Reality House, Project Aquarius, and the Always a Better Cause group.

When not on location for a movie, Eastwood and his wife spend their time with a few close friends, including Malpaso producer Bob Daley; an actor friend, Cissy Donner; Fritz Manes, who works for an Oakland television station; dentist Don Kincade, also a high school friend who lives in Davis, California, and a few others Eastwood has met in Carmel. His closest show-business friends are Don Siegel and Merv Griffin, who lives near Eastwood.

He does spend some of his time with various Eastwood enterprises such as the Hog's Breath Inn, a restaurant he partly owns in Carmel.

But Eastwood's primary commitment is to the movies.

"I love acting," he has said, "and I intend to continue doing it. But I must admit that the satisfaction of directing goes deeper than any other facet of film making. In direction you are responsible for the entire concept of the telling of a story; in acting you are mainly concerned with your own interpretation of one of the characters in the plot."

"But I suppose my involvement goes even deeper than acting or directing. I love every aspect of the creation of a motion picture, and I guess I'm committed to it for life."

It may be ironically fitting that the last word should go to Pauline Kael, the reviewer who has been the most hostile to Eastwood and his films. In her review of *Magnum Force* in *The New*

*Yorker*, Kael, in attempting to belittle the contribution of Clint Eastwood, may very well have paid him a meaningful tribute.

"Eastwood," she wrote, "isn't very different from many of the traditional inexpressive stalward heroes of Westerns and cops-and-robbers films—actors notoriously devoid of personality—but the change in action films can be seen in its purest form in him."

"Eastwood," she continued, "stands melodrama on its head; in his world nice guys finish last. This is no longer the romantic world in which the hero is, fortunately, the best shot; instead, the best shot is the hero. And that could be what the American audience for action films, grown derisive about the triumph of the good, was waiting for. Eastwood's gun power makes him the hero of a totally nihilistic dream world."

# Filmography

From 1955 to 1958 Clint Eastwood appeared as a bit player in Universal-International pictures, generally uncredited. He does receive credits in the following films made during this period for Universal and other studios:

### 1955 *REVENGE OF THE CREATURE*
### (shot in 3-D)

Director: Jack Arnold
Producer: Universal-International
Screenplay: Martin Berkeley (from a story by William Alland)
Director of Photography: Charles S. Welbourne
Cast: John Agar (Professor Clete Ferguson), Lori Nelson (Helen Dobson), John Bromfield (Joe Hayes), Nestor Paiva (Lucas), Grandon Rhodes (Jackson Foster), Dave Willock (Lou Gibson), Clint Eastwood (Jennings), Robert B. Williams (George Johnson), Charles Cane (Police Captain)

## 1955 *FRANCIS IN THE NAVY*

Director: Arthur Lubin
Producer: Universal-International
Screenplay: Devery Freeman
Director of Photography: Carl Guthrie
Cast: Donald O'Connor (Lt. Peter Stirling and Slicker Donavan), Martha Hyer (Betsy Donavan), Richard Erdman (Murph), Jim Backus (Commander Hutch), David Janssen (Lt. Anders), Clint Eastwood (Jonesy), Martin Milner (Rick), Paul Burke (Tate)

## 1955 *LADY GODIVA*

Director: Arthur Lubin
Producer: Universal-International
Screenplay: Oscar Brodney and Harry Ruskin
Director of Photography: Carl Guthrie
Cast: Maureen O'Hara (Godiva), George Nader (Leofric), Victor McLaglen (Grimald), Rex Reason (Harold), Torin Thatcher (Godwin). Eastwood had a small role as a Saxon. Paul Brinegar, who appeared with Eastwood later in *Rawhide* as Wishbone, the cook, also had a small role in the film.

## 1955 *TARANTULA*

Director: Jack Arnold
Producer: Universal-International

Screenplay: Robert M. Fresco and Martin Berkeley
Director of Photography: George Robinson
Cast: John Agar, Mara Corday, Leo G. Carroll, Nestor Paiva. Eastwood appeared briefly in the film as a pilot. (In *Coogan's Bluff* during the discothèque scene, one of the images projected on the giant screen is that of a spider. The shot is taken from *Tarantula*.)

## 1956 *NEVER SAY GOODBYE*

Director: Jerry Hopper
Producer: Universal-International
Screenplay: Charles Hoffman
Director of Photography: Maury Gertsman
Cast: Rock Hudson (Dr. Michael Carrington), Cornell Borchers (Lisa), George Sanders (Victor), Ray Collins (Dr. Bailey), David Janssen (Dave). Eastwood had a small role as Will.

## 1956 *THE FIRST TRAVELING SALESLADY*

Director: Arthur Lubin
Producer: RKO
Screenplay: Devery Freeman and Stephen Longstreet
Director of Photography: William Snyder
Cast: Ginger Rogers (Rose Gillray), Barry Nelson (Charles Masters), Carol Channing (Molly Wade), Brian Keith (James Carter),

James Arness (Joel Kingdon), Clint Eastwood (Jack Rice). (Credits for the film
read "introducing Clint Eastwood.")

## 1956 *STAR IN THE DUST*

Director: Charles Haas
Producer: Universal-International
Screenplay: Oscar Brodney
Director of Photography: John L. Russell,
Jr.
Cast: John Agar (Sheriff Bill Jordan), Ma-
mie Van Doren (Ellen Ballard), Richard
Boone (Sam Hall), Leif Erickson (George
Ballard), Coleen Gray (Nellie Mason),
Paul Fix (Mike MacNamara), Harry Mor-
gan (Lew Hogan). Eastwood had a small
role as a ranchhand.

## 1957 *ESCAPADE IN JAPAN*

Director: Arthur Lubin
Producer: RKO
Screenplay: Winston Miller
Director of Photography: William Snyder
Cast: Teresa Wright (Mary Saunders),
Cameron Mitchell (Dick Saunders), Jon
Provost (Tony Saunders), Roger Nakagawa
(Hiko). Eastwood had one line as the pilot
of a plane looking for a lost boy.

1958 *AMBUSH AT CIMARRON PASS*

Director: Jodie Copelan
Producer: Twentieth Century Fox (Jodie Copelan)
Screenplay: Richard G. Taylor and John K. Butler
Director of Photography: John M. Nickolaus, Jr.
Cast: Scott Brady (Sgt. Matt Blake), Margia Dean (Teresa), Clint Eastwood (Keith Williams), Irving Bacon (Stanfield)

1958 *LAFAYETTE ESCADRILLE*

Director: William Wellman
Producer: William Wellman (Warner Bros.)
Screenplay: A. S. Fleischman (from a story by William Wellman)
Director of Photography: William Clothier
Cast: Tab Hunter (Thad Walker), Etchika Choureau (Rennee Beaulieu), Marcel Dalio (Drillmaster), Bill Wellman, Jr. (Bill Wellman), Jody McCrea (Tom Hitchcock), Dennis Devine (Red Scanlon), David Janssen (Duke Sinclaire), Paul Fix (U.S. General), Veloa Vonns (The Madam), Will Hutchins (Dave Putnam), Clint Eastwood (George Moseley), Tom Laughlin (Arthur Bluthenthal)

In 1958 and 1959 Eastwood appeared in a number of television shows, including *Highway Patrol, Navy Log, Maverick, Men of Annapolis,* and *West Point,* a syndicated series in which he had a continuing role for the first few episodes.

January 9, 1959, to February 8, 1966, Eastwood did 250 one-hour *Rawhide* television shows for CBS. All were on film. For the last 22 episodes, Eastwood was the sole star. The series starred Eric Fleming as Gil Favor, Eastwood as Rowdy Yates, Paul Brinnegeɪ as Wishbone.

## 1964 *A FISTFUL OF DOLLARS*

Director: Sergio Leone
Producer: Harry Colombo, George Papi (Arrigo Colombo and Giorgio Papi) (U.S.: United Artists)
Screenplay: Sergio Leone and Duccio Tessari (based upon the Japanese film *Yojimbo*)
Director of Photography: Jack Dalmas (Massimo Dallamano)
Cast: Clint Eastwood (The Stranger), Gian Maria Volonté (Ramon Rojo), Mariane Koch (Marisol), Pepe Calvo (Silvanito), Wolfgang Lukschy (John Baxter), Sieghardt Rupp (Estaban Rojo), Antonion Prieto (Benito Rojo)

## 1965 *FOR A FEW DOLLARS MORE*

Director: Sergio Leone
Producer: Alberto Grimaldi (U.S.: United Artists)

Screenplay: Luciano Vincenzoni and Sergio
Leone
Director of Photography: Massimo Dalla-
mano
Cast: Clint Eastwood (The Stranger), Lee
Van Cleef (Colonel Mortimer), Gian Maria
Volonté (El Indio), Klaus Kinski (Hunch-
back).

## 1966 *THE GOOD, THE BAD, AND THE UGLY*

Director: Sergio Leone
Producer: Alberto Grimaldi (U.S.: United
Artists)
Screenplay: Luciano Vincenzoni and Sergio
Leone
Director of Photography: Tonnio Delli
Colli
Cast: Clint Eastwood (The Stranger, also
known as Blondie or Joe), Eli Wallach
(Tuco), Lee Van Cleef (Stenza, also known
as Angel Eyes).

The distinctive music for all three of the
Eastwood-Leone films was composed and
conducted by Ennio Morricone, who also
composed and conducted the music for
*Two Mules for Sister Sara.*

## 1967 *THE WITCHES* (Episode entitled "A Night Like Any Other").

Director: Vittorio De Sica
Producer: Dino De Laurentiis

Screenplay: Casare Zavattini, Faboi Carpi, Enzio Muzil
Director of Photography: Giuseppe Maccari, Giuseppe Rotunno
Cast: Clint Eastwood, Silvana Mangano

(The film was in five parts with five directors and five casts.)

## 1968 *HANG 'EM HIGH*

Director: Ted Post
Producer: Leonard Freeman (United Artists )
Screenplay: Leonard Freeman and Mel Goldberg
Director of Photography: Leonard South and Richard Kline
Cast: Clint Eastwood (Jed Cooper), Inger Stevens (Rachel), Ed Begley (Cap'n Wilson), Pat Hingle (Judge Fenton), Charles McGraw (Sherrif Ray Calhoun), Ruth White (Madame Sophie), Arlene Golonka (Jennifer), James MacArthur (The Preacher), Bruce Dern (Miller), Alan Hale, Jr. (Stone), James Westerfield (Prisoner), L.Q. Jones (Hangman)

## 1969 *COOGAN'S BLUFF*

Director: Don Siegel
Producer: Don Siegel (Universal)
Exec. Producer: Richard Lyons
Screenplay: Herman Miller, Dean Riesner,

and Howard Rodman, from a story by Herman Miller

Cinematographer: Bud Thackery

Editor: Sam Waxman

Art Directors: Alexander Golitzen and Robert C. MacKichan

Sets: John McCarthy and John Austin

Assistant Director: Joe Cavalier

Dialogue Coach: Scott Hale

Music: Lalo Schifrin

Cast: Clint Eastwood (Coogan), Lee J. Cobb (McElroy), Susan Clark (Julie), Tisha Sterling (Linny Raven), Don Stroud (Ringerman), Betty Field (Mrs. Ringerman), Tom Tully (Sherriff McCrea), Melodie Johnson (Millie), James Edwards (Jackson), Rudy Diaz (Running Bear), David F. Doyle (Pushie), Louis Zorich (Taxi Driver), Meg Myles (Big Red), Marjorie Bennett (Mrs. Fowler), Seymour Cassel (Young Hood), John Coe (Bellboy), Skip Battyn, Albert Popwell, Conrad Bain, James Gavin, Albert Henderson, James McCallion, Syl Lamont, Jess Osuna, Jerry Summers, Antonia Rey, Marya Henriques

1969 *WHERE EAGLES DARE*

Director: Brian Hutton

Producer: Elliott Kastner (MGM)

Screenplay: Alistair MacLean (based on his novel)

Director of Photography: Arthur Ibbeston

Cast: Richard Burton (John Smith), Clint

Eastwood (Lt. Morris Schaffer), Mary Ure (Mary Ellison), Michael Hordern (Vice-Admiral Rolland), Patrick Wymark (Col. Wyatt Turner), Robert Beatty (Cartwright-Jones), Anton Diffring (Col. Kramer), Donald Houston (Olaf Christiansen).

## 1969 *PAINT YOUR WAGON*

Director: Joshua Logan
Producer: (Paramount) Alan Jay Lerner
Screenplay: Alan Jay Lerner and Paddy Chayefsky
Director of Photography: William A. Fraker
Cast: Lee Marvin (Ben Rumson), Clint Eastwood (Pardner), Jean Seberg (Elizabeth), Harve Presnell (Rotten Luck Willie), Ray Walston (Mad Jack Duncan)

## 1970 *KELLY'S HEROES*

Director: Brian Hutton
Producer: Katzka-Loeb-MGM
Screenplay: Troy Kennedy Martin
Director of Photography: Gabriel Figueroa
Cast: Clint Eastwood (Kelly), Telly Savalas (Sergeant), Don Rickles (Quartermaster), Donald Sutherland (Oddball), Carroll O'Connor (General), Gavin MacLeod, Hall Buckley, Stuart Margolin, Jeff Morris, Richard Davalos.

Director: Donald Siegel
Producer: Martin Rackin (Universal)
Screenplay: Albert Maltz, from a story by Budd Boetticher
Cinematographer: Gabriel Figueroa
Editor: Robert Shugrue
Art Director: Jose Rodriguez Granada
2nd Unit Director: Joe Cavalier
Sets: Pablo Galvan
Music: Ennio Morricone
Dialogue Coach: Leon Charles
Assistant Directors: Joe Cavalier and Manuel Munoz
Cast: Clint Eastwood (Hogan), Shirley MacLaine (Sister Sara), Manolo Fabregas (Col. Beltran), Alberto Morin, Armando, Silvestre, Jose Chavez, Pedro Galvan, Jose Angel Espinosa, Enrique Lucero, Aurora Munoz, Xavier Marc, Hortensia Santovena, Rosa Furman, Jose Torvay, Margarita Luna, Javier Masse

## 1971 *THE BEGUILED*

Director: Don Siegel
Producer: Don Siegel (Universal)
Screenplay: John B. Sherry and Grimes Grice (Albert Maltz), from the novel by Thomas Cullinan
Cinematographer: Bruce Surtees
Editor: Carl Pingitore
Production Designer: Ted Haworth

Art Director: Alexander Golitzen
2nd Unit Director: Joe Cavalier
Sets: John Austin
Dialogue Coach: Scott Hale
Music: Lalo Schifrin
Cast: Clint Eastwood (John McBurney),
Geraldine Page (Martha), Elizabeth Hartman (Edwina), Jo Ann Harris (Carol),
Darleen Carr (Doris), Mae Mercer (Hallie), Pamelyn Ferdin (Amy), Melody Thomas (Abigail), Peggy Drier (Lizzie),
Patty Mattick (Janie)

## 1971 *PLAY MISTY FOR ME*

Director: Clint Eastwood
Producer: Robert Daley (Malpaso-Universal)
Screenplay: Jo Heims and Dean Riesner (from a story by Jo Heims)
Director of Photography: Bruce Surtees
Cast: Clint Eastwood (Dave Garland),
Jessica Walter (Evelyn Draper), Donna
Mills (Tobie Williams), John Larch (Sgt.
McCallum), Jack Ging (Dr. Frank Dewan),
Irene Hervey (Madge Brenner), James
McEachin (Al Monte), Clarice Taylor
(Birdie), Donald Siegel (Murphy the Bartender)

## 1971 *DIRTY HARRY*

Director: Don Siegel
Producer: Don Siegel (Warner Bros.)

Exec. Producer: Robert Daley
Assoc. Producer: Carl Pingitore
Screenplay: Harry Julian Fink, R. M. Fink,
and Dean Riesner, from a story by Harry
Julian Fink and R. M. Fink
Cinematographer: Bruce Surtees
Editor: Carl Pingitore
Art Director: Dale Hennessey
Music: Lalo Schifrin
Dialogue Supervisor: Scott Hale
Cast: Clint Eastwood (Harry), Harry
Guardino (Bressler), Andy Robinson (The
Killer), Reni Santoni (Chico), John Vernon
(The Mayor), John Larch (Police Chief),
John Mitchum (DeGeorgio), Mae Mercer
(Mrs. Russell), Lyn Edgington (Norma),
Ruth Kobart (Bus Driver), Woodrow Par-
frey (Mr. Jaffe), Josef Sommer (Rothko),
William Paterson (Bannerman), James No-
lan (Liquor Store Proprietor), Maurice S.
Argent (Sid Kleinman), Joe de Winter
(Miss Willow), Craig G. Kelly (Sgt. Re-
ineke)

1972 *JOE KIDD*

Director: John Sturges
Producer: Malpaso-Universal (Robert
Daley)
Screenplay: Elmore Leonard
Director of Photography: Bruce Surgees
Cast: Clint Eastwood (Joe Kidd), John
Saxon (Luis Chama), Robert Duvall, Stella
Garcia, Don Stroud, James Wainright

1972 *HIGH PLAINS DRIFTER*

Director: Clint Eastwood
Producer: Robert Daley (Universal-Malpaso)
Screenplay: Ernest Tidyman
Director of Photography: Bruce Surtees
Cast: Clint Eastwood (The Stranger), Verna Bloom (Sarah Belding), Mariana Hill (Callie Travers), Mitchell Ryan (Dave Drake), Jack Ging (Morgan Allen), Stefan Gierasch (Mayor Jason Hobart), Ted Hartley (Lewis Belding), Billy Curtis (Mordecai), Geoffrey Lewis (Stacey Bridges), Paul Brinager (Luttie Naylor)

1973 *BREEZY*

Director: Clint Eastwood
Producer: Robert Daley (Universal)
Screenplay: Jo Heims
Director of Photography: Frank Stanley
Cast: William Holden (Frank Harmon), Kay Lenz (Breezy), Roger C. Carmel (Bob Henderson), Marj Dusay (Betty), Joan Hotchkis (Paula), Jamie Smith Jackson (Marcy), Norman Bartold (Man in Car), Lynn Borden (Overnight Date), Shelley Morrison (Nancy)

1973 *MAGNUM FORCE*

Director: Ted Post
Producer: Robert Daley (Warner Bros.)

Screenplay: John Milius and Michael Cimino (story by John Milius)
Director of Photography: Frank Stanley
Cast: Clint Eastwood (Harry Callahan), Hal Holbrook (Lt. Briggs), Mitchell Ryan (McCoy), David Soul (David), Felton Perry (Early Smith)


## 1974 *THUNDERBOLT AND LIGHTFOOT*

Director: Michael Cimino
Director of Photography: Frank Stanley
Producer: Robert Daley (Malpaso-United Artists)
Screenplay: Michael Cimino
Director of Photography: Frank Stanley
Cast: Clint Eastwood (Thunderbolt), Jeff Bridges (Lightfoot), George Kennedy (Red Leary), Geoffrey Lewis (Goody)

## 1974 *THE EIGER SANCTION*

Producer: Robert Daley. Executive Producers Richard D. Zanuck & David Brown. (Malpaso-Universal).